ALSO BY KAY ALLENBAUGH

Chocolate for a Woman's Soul

Chocolate for a Woman's Heart

Chocolate for a Lover's Heart

Chocolate for a Mother's Heart

Chocolate for a Woman's Spirit

Chocolate for a Teen's Soul

77 Heartwarming Stories

of Gratitude That Celebrate

the Good Things in Life

A FIRESIDE BOOK
Published by Simon & Schuster
New York   London   Toronto   Sydney   Singapore

CHOCOLATE
for a
WOMAN'S
BLESSINGS

KAY ALLENBAUGH

FIRESIDE
Rockefeller Center
1230 Avenue of the Americas
New York, NY 10020

FIRESIDE and colophon are registered trademarks
of Simon & Schuster, Inc.

Manufactured in the United States of America

1   3   5   7   9   10   8   6   4   2

Library of Congress Cataloging-in-Publication Data
Chocolate for a woman's blessings : 77 heartwarming
stories of gratitude that celebrate the good things in life /
[compiled by] Kay Allenbaugh.
p. cm.
"A Fireside book."
1. Women—Religious life.   I. Allenbaugh, Kay.
BJ1610 .C47   2001
291.4'32—dc21
00-058846
ISBN 0-7432-0308-9

This book is dedicated to women everywhere

who count their blessings, thereby

creating a positive ripple effect for all the lives

they touch.

CONTENTS

III

OUR FAVORITE FURRY ONES

IV

THE ANSWERS ARE WITHIN

V

SOME KIND OF WONDERFUL

VI

ONE STEP AT A TIME

VII

HOLIDAYS, HOPE, AND HOLLY

VIII

TOUGH ON ISSUES, SOFT ON PEOPLE

IX

KEEPING THE MEMORIES ALIVE

X

DANCING WITH ANGELS

XI

LIFE'S LITTLE IRONIES

INTRODUCTION

When I began this book, I realized that I needed to figure out what I meant by "blessings." I thought of all the things I love about my own life. But the more I thought, the more I realized that the things I'm truly grateful for are the things for which I've worked hardest.

Each of us can easily bring to mind the most challenging times we've faced—like recovering from a serious illness or accident, struggling to get the education or the job we want, dealing with a painful loss, or healing from a betrayal. Ironically, the chances we are given to work through hardship oftentimes bring us the best gifts of all—peace and joy.

Chocolate for a Woman's Blessings shows us the ways that many women have found that peace and joy. Inspirational stories are themselves like chocolate—they warm our hearts and lift our spirits. They make us feel good. Even better, stories like these remind us of who we really are! I am blessed that seventy-four elegant women have shared their poignant, true stories in *Chocolate for a Woman's Blessings*. Many of the storytellers in this book are inspirational speakers, consultants, therapists, writers, and best-selling authors. These women have examined their blessings and have discovered the infinite joys of living. Like chocolate itself, these stories delight, comfort, and satisfy as they encourage us to look at the abundance in our own lives and view every challenge as an opportunity.

Savoring each story in *Chocolate for a Woman's Blessings* is the perfect opportunity to pause, get quiet, and be thankful for all that you have and for all the good that is yet to come. I believe that whatever we pay attention to expands. By possessing a grateful spirit—counting our blessings on a regular basis—and being there for ourselves and others, we enrich our lives. The stories in *Chocolate for a Woman's Blessings* trace the journey of many grateful hearts as they share varied tales of learning, loving, and laughing, while celebrating all the good things that add up to a full life.

And if this is a time in your life when it is difficult for you to believe that countless blessings are heading your way, let the "Chocolate sisters" believe it into existence for you—until you know it to be so for yourself.

I
ON HIGHER GROUND

There is no support so strong as the strength

that enables one to stand alone.

Ellen Glasgow

GOODIE BAGS FROM THE HEART

Nineteen years old and newly married. I remember waving goodbye to my husband one hot summer day while standing on the front porch of our small home in California. As I stood outside, I noticed the saddest sight across the street in the fast-food parking lot. He appeared to be homeless in his grubby, dirty clothes and long gray hair. In the heat of the day, he wore a tattered black jacket that I'm sure must have been one of his most treasured possessions that kept him warm in the cooler months. His fiercely thick gray beard hid part of his face, and frankly he looked quite frightening to me. I quickly turned and stepped into the house, shutting and locking the door behind me.

As I stood at my living room window staring in bewilderment, he rummaged through the garbage cans in the parking lot. Wrappers, cups, napkins—he went through all of it in hopes of finding food, and when he did find a morsel or two, it looked as though he had found a Thanksgiving dinner. Not feeling afraid any longer, I wondered just how long it had been since this poor man had had a decent meal.

The next day while sending my husband off to work, I spotted the man again. He was sitting on the curb with cups and wrappers in his lap, eagerly eating the unwanted scraps of strangers as if there were no tomorrow. I couldn't help but feel sorry for him, and it was at that very moment that I knew what I had to do, and I hoped that my plan would work.

The next day I found myself packing two lunches instead of just the usual one for my husband, and thinking to myself, *Oh, I hope he shows up.* When I finished my task, I hurried across the hot pavement and slipped one of the brown paper bags into the garbage can. I laughed to myself and thought, *Boy, I must look like I'm up to something strange.* I sent my husband to work and quickly went to the living room window to watch and wait for my homeless friend.

In a matter of minutes he arrived and immediately found the sack with the lunch inside. I stood there with a huge smile on my face, my heart pounding as he opened the bag and peered inside. He sat down on the curb of the busy intersection happily eating his lunch, oblivious to the passing cars just feet in front of him. He munched contentedly on a bologna sandwich, chips, a soda, and whatever other goodies I had happened to find in my cupboard that morning.

We didn't have much money or food back then, just starting out as a young couple. But for the next two weeks I scrounged through my kitchen cupboards and always managed to find something to slip into a goodie bag for the old man. And, of course, I placed it in the very same garbage can every day. I watched him savor every bite day after day, and it did my heart a world of good.

I used to wonder if he thought it was odd having lunches appear, but he never once looked around in curiosity. Then one day I slipped a lunch into the garbage can and he failed to show up, and I worried about him. I said a prayer for him in hopes that he had just decided it was time to move on.

Years later, when I was thirty-four years old, my children, ages eight, ten, ten, and twelve, were teasing me one day, saying, "Mom, name one good deed you've ever done." My face lit up, and I knew at that moment what I would say.

PAULA J. TOYNBEE

JOANNA

*S*he came too early—willing her way into the world with the sheer force of her being.

"Too small" they told us. "She may be too small to survive." At just over two and a half pounds, they were right. Twenty-six years ago a two-and-a-half-pound baby didn't stand much of a chance.

But it wasn't fair. She had fought so hard to live—had defied the odds already merely by surviving her abrupt entry into harsh lights, cold air, and oxygen. Thanks to a cesarean section she was spared the agonizingly slow journey to the light down the dark, narrow tunnel of the birth canal, and now she was here—so tiny and ill-equipped and yet so determined to live.

I left the hospital a week later without her. The emptiness in my womb was nothing compared to the hollow shell that was my heart. I had left my baby. Left her there held captive inside a tiny, Lucite bassinet hooked up to wires and tubes. In spite of it all, though, she was beautiful, with bright red lips and thick dark hair. She was a miniature baby. Perfect in every detail, but oh so tiny.

Every day, twice a day, I made the long trip to the hospital and home again with aching arms and swollen eyes that endlessly poured tears. There was no stopping the tears. They came all the while I tried so hard to be cheerful for the child at home, Adam, the healthy four-year-old who himself was trying so desperately to be patient and not ask too often when his new baby sister was coming home.

For two months my child balanced herself precariously between life and death. For two months my husband, Howard, and I tiptoed around the subject, never asking each other, or even ourselves, the unspoken question, the "what if" we knew we couldn't face.

Two months in the hospital with thousands and thousands of dollars' worth of unpaid bills covering the desk top in the den. Who cared what it cost? What did money matter? This was my child. My infant whom I couldn't even hold to my breast for an entire month for fear that I would disrupt the precious lifeline of oxygen that snaked its way soundlessly into her bassinet. Each time I looked at her my breasts, dried now of the milk that was so rightfully hers, my body, my entire soul was racked with the pain of the impossibility of the situation. We were kept from each other. Kept from bonding. Unable to touch through the boundaries of glass and metal that surrounded and sustained her.

Finally after two long months, we were told that we could take her home. She weighed four pounds eleven ounces and had to eat every four hours, twenty-four hours around the clock. We were also told that all of her reflexes were not fully developed yet and sometimes she couldn't suck, breathe, and swallow at the same time. It seems that given the choice of food over air she always chose food (obviously my child), and invariably, at least twice a day, during feeding she turned bright blue and passed out. "And, oh, by the way," they mentioned as we made our way toward the door, "she might be retarded. Just keep an eye on her. See if you notice anything unusual."

And so we took our teeny bundle home. How she didn't drown in my tears that day I will never know. Howard and I both wept all the way home. Be careful what you wish for. All I asked for, prayed for, all this time was to bring our baby home. I had gotten my wish but at what cost?

Early evening on my first full day home with my baby the

doorbell rang. I panicked. There I was at five-thirty in the afternoon still in my nightgown. The sink was filled with breakfast and lunch dishes, and my four-year-old was sitting, dazed, in front of the TV. I had managed to neutralize him with an overdose of sugar and four hours of straight TV in order to give myself time to attend to the baby's constant demands. They had told us to feed her every four hours but they had neglected to tell us that it would take an hour and a half to get two ounces down her tiny gullet. Even then, when we were successful at that, she managed to vomit one and a half ounces back up. By the time I fed her, changed her, put her down, and made my way back to bed, it was just about time to start again.

I didn't even remember if I had brushed my teeth that day but I was past caring. I opened the door and there was my pediatrician, standing there with a big smile—his medical bag in one hand and a pizza in the other. I just stared, astounded.

"I was just on my way home," he said (I knew it was a lie; he lived ten miles in the opposite direction), "so I thought I'd stop by. How's the baby doing?"

I burst into tears. Somehow he managed to maneuver me, the baby, the little black bag, and the pizza—half pepperoni, half mushroom—into the kitchen. He sat me down, popped the pizza into the oven, and set the baby in the infant seat on the floor. While he rocked the infant seat with his foot he proceeded to wash the dishes in the sink.

"I'm just going to examine her. Why don't you jump into the shower; you'll feel better."

I couldn't believe it. When I came out, Adam was fed and happily chatting with his doctor and the baby was sound asleep.

Dr. Markman left soon after, but at least once a week for the next three months his visits would be repeated. Sometimes it was Kentucky Fried Chicken or Taco Bell, but whatever the food, it was always accompanied by his warm smile and a shoulder to cry on as we cheered Joanna to good health.

There was never a bill for those house calls, and it was a good thing, because there was no amount of money that could have adequately compensated him for the kindness he showered on me.

Judi Sadowsky

MADE FOR WATER

Mom took me to my Aunt Marilyn's house to be watched while she went to work. I was afraid of that woman, who was larger than anyone is ever supposed to be, and I cried the entire way, every day, down the cracked narrow sidewalk to her house. The wind blew hard on my face, pushing me back. My mother pressed on, dragging me by the hand—around the corner, past the church on the left, and straight up to my aunt's front door.

My mother knocked, and I hid behind her. Aunt Marilyn's slow, heavy steps vibrated under my feet as I heard her coming to the door: *thud, thud, thud*—like the dinosaur in *Jurassic Park*. The door swung open and my aunt's pungent aroma—a unique, acidic scent—rushed out. *That's the way you smell when you're fat*, I thought. The smell rushed out the door and into my nose, but it didn't stop there. It wrapped itself around my body, grabbed me, and pulled me inside her house.

A talented artist, she spent much of her time in front of an easel. While she skillfully placed thick, luxuriant layers of paint onto her canvas, I contemplated her unique features. She had long black hair that almost reached her waist, and enormous round feet. She was barefoot most of the time because they don't make shoes that big. Her paintings depicted vivid landscapes, full of texture and life. *How does she know how to paint them?* I wondered. Had she ever been that far from her weary kitchen chair?

At lunchtime, we often ate giant cheese sandwiches toasted

golden brown. I watched in fascination as the orange ribbon stretched out between the chunk in my mouth and the chunk in my hand. My throat felt tight. I ate small, timid bites. I knew food like that made you fat—then you smelled, and had to go barefoot, and had to wear skirts you sewed yourself because they don't make skirts that big. My fear of the woman was nothing compared to my fear of becoming her. I tried to hide it, but the way she looked at me, I think she knew.

Sometimes, I went to the bathroom out of boredom. I lounged on the toilet and stared into the stained porcelain bowl, my thighs flattened out against the cold rim. I estimated that each thigh was as big around as one of Aunt Marilyn's wrists, and I sat upright in horror. If one of Aunt Marilyn's thighs was as big around as my whole body, then how could she fit onto the toilet? I eyed the freestanding bathtub; no way could she wedge her coagulated mass into that! Could she even fit through the narrow doorway? I ran from the room in terror.

On hot summer days, my mother and my aunt took all of us cousins out to Ash Lake for a day of swimming and picnicking. I couldn't swim yet, but I liked to pretend I could. I propelled myself through the water by pushing off the muddy lake bottom as each armstroke completed its downward motion through the water. I kicked, splashed, and basked in the sun-warmed shallows while the other children swam and our mothers relaxed on the shore, talking.

It was there, amid the sounds of conversation and laughter, that I found out the truth about Aunt Marilyn.

Aunt Marilyn stood up and began to wade out into the lake. The water parted behind her in a wide V, and she walked slowly, resolutely, placing each step firmly on the muddy lake floor. She was thigh-high in the water, but she didn't stop there. She plodded on, past where I could reach the bottom, out to where the water reached the exact middle of her body. Her colossal skirt billowed above the water like a hot-air balloon preparing for liftoff. I looked wildly around me, marveling that no one tried to stop her. Aunt Marilyn was in imminent danger, but no one else seemed to notice the sudden chill in the air.

Aunt Marilyn smoothed her skirt down into the murky water. She leaned back, kicked up her elephantine feet, and floated.

Aunt Marilyn floated!

Goose bumps covered my arms and shoulders. No way to pee, no way to bathe, no shoes to wear; yet my Aunt Marilyn could float better than anyone I'd ever seen. Her body barely immersed, she rose above the water like a majestic, fleshy ship. A rare smile rested on her face as she drifted effortlessly around the lake, finally at home.

I realized then that Aunt Marilyn was not made for land; she was made for water.

She stayed out there for hours while the rest of us played near the shore. I scanned the lake often, and each time I would find her floating in a patch of sunlight with the smooth water cradling her body. The beauty of that sight transformed me. Gazing at my aunt, I felt that all was right in the world. I was warm and safe. I knew where I belonged.

When the sun had lowered in the sky, Aunt Marilyn returned to us begrudgingly. She forced her mass through the reluctant water. Each step thudded down into the mud, which formed a suction around her feet, begging her to stay. Somehow, she dragged herself out onto the land, where she weighed more than anyone is ever supposed to weigh. She came out of the water, and the water came with her—gallons of it ran off her skirt as she gathered it into her powerful hands and wrung it out.

Aunt Marilyn looked up and saw me staring at her. Her large, sad eyes bore into mine, and I noticed for the first time how beautiful they were. Her eyes were the color of the sky, softened by a layer of thin, wispy clouds. I swallowed hard, overwhelmed by the strangeness of my new understanding, and I continued to stare reverently at that captivating creature who belonged to the water. I shook with admiration, no longer awed by her size—but awed by her strength. The way she looked at me, I think she knew.

Aunt Marilyn let me see one lonely tear trek its way down her weathered cheek. One tear and that was all. Then she took my hand and together we walked back to the station wagon. Her soft hand tenderly encircled mine; I was grateful for its warmth.

If I could travel back in time, I would do one thing differently. I'd take a ride around Ash Lake with my aunt—the way the other kids remember doing. Perched lightly on top of her belly, I'm quite sure I could have shouted with absolute authority, "We are the Queens of the World!"

LUCI N. FULLER

KEVIN AND THE SAINT

"*Santa for special kids on tomorrow's broadcast. See you then.*"

The tag line caught my attention. I raised my head from my book and saw a picture of a waving Santa on the television screen as the Channel 6 news credits rolled by. My heart began to pound. Could this be the Santa I'd been looking for?

I picked up the phone and called the station. "That Santa tomorrow, can he communicate with deaf children?" I asked.

Over the rumble of the newsroom, I heard, "Yes, he's a retired schoolteacher who signs. He won't release his name, but he's scheduled to be at the Memphis city mall tomorrow. We'll be picking up the story through our affiliate news station."

"Memphis? You mean Tennessee, not in Florida?"

"Yes, can I help you with anything else?" He was pressuring me to end the conversation.

"No, thank you." I hung up, disappointed.

Just then Jessica came into the office. Her face changed after seeing my saddened expression. "What's wrong?"

"You know I love your son like a nephew, right?"

She smiled. "Of course. You're his favorite babysitter."

"Well, I'd like to take him to Tennessee tomorrow to the Memphis mall. There's a Santa who knows sign language scheduled to appear."

A twinkle sparkled in her eyes. "Kevin's six. He doesn't need to visit Santa Claus anymore. That's really sweet of you to think of him. But I'd rather instill in him the true meaning of Christmas, Jesus' birth, not just exchanging presents."

My heart broke. I wanted her to know how much it would mean to Kevin. He'd never met a Santa who could understand him. Last year when we took him to our local mall, he signed his name to the Santa there.

"Yes, I'll bring you that," the Santa had replied.

Kevin had cried for hours. He decided Santa didn't give gifts to children who couldn't speak. *That isn't good enough, not for Kevin,* I thought. He deserved a Santa who could relate.

"You really want to drive all that way just so he can tell him he wants a Pokémon?"

"Santa isn't just a man in a red suit," I explained. "He's the spirit of giving. He's Jesus' helper, spreading cheer to all the little girls and boys, even the deaf ones. For the first time Kevin will be able to think Santa knows who he is."

She nodded. "Well, all right, we'll go tonight. Bring a map and your camera?"

"Of course." I happily laughed. "We have to make a memento!"

Later in the evening Kevin piled into the minivan clutching his pillow.

His mother signed, "Don't you want to see Saint Nick?"

Kevin moved his fingers. "He doesn't like me unless I write."

"That's not true," his mother mouthed slowly.

Soon, Kevin snuggled in his backseat bed as mile after mile drifted by. Palm trees and scrub brush gave way to reddened clay. We drove until the air chilled and the land grew hilly.

I wasn't sure if I was overstepping my bounds, but I hoped this would be a wonderful experience for Kevin. He deserved to communicate with Santa.

When we arrived early the next afternoon at the mall, his

mother signed to Kevin, who was staring back at her, "We're here."

Wiggling in anticipation, he signed, "Do you think Santa cares that I came?"

I looked around at all the cars and knew enough to nod my head yes.

Kevin jumped out of the minivan and took his mother's hand and mine. Together we walked through the crowded walkways to the open courtyard. There, on top of a platform, was an older man with real gray hair. His stomach looked pillow-plumped, but there was no mistaking his outfit of red and white. He sat enthroned next to a sparkling, bedecked Christmas tree.

His mother gestured, "That's him, straight from the North Pole."

Kevin's eyes suddenly lit up at the whole Yule scene. He vaulted up the steps and stood in front of Santa. His mother and I scampered to catch up. By the time we got to Santa's chair, Kevin was signing, "I'm Kevin Johnson from Orlando, Florida."

"Hello, Kevin. You live near Disney World," Santa signed back. "You've been very good this year. What would you like for Christmas. Let me guess . . . a Pokémon?"

I knew that was probably what all the little boys had asked Santa for, but Kevin's eyes lit up as if Santa knew him personally.

"You're the real Santa," Kevin signed.

"Anything else?" the smiling, rosy-cheeked Santa asked.

Kevin quickly moved his hands to cross his chest.

Knowing what Kevin wanted, Santa stretched his arms to give a giant hug.

Tears came to my eyes as I raised my camera to capture the moment. Truly this anonymous Santa embodied the spirit of giving. This retired schoolteacher gave his heart to the children who weren't like everyone else, the ones who needed to communicate in their own way.

All children are special, I know that, but seeing Kevin hug Santa reminded me of how important every individual is. Whenever I look at my framed picture of Santa hugging Kevin, I want to thank him for a memory that will never fade for Kevin, his family, and me.

MICHELE WALLACE CAMPANELLI

DRIVING DENNY

During our forty-nine years of marriage, Denny was rarely a passenger in our car. Wherever we went, he drove and I rode along. It was that simple. No questions asked. A mutual assumption had been made by both of us so long ago that I forgot the reason. But this driving arrangement was about to change forever.

One year ago, Denny was diagnosed with a fast-growing cancer requiring such aggressive treatments that he was often too ill to drive. That is when I became his official chauffeur. It also reminded me of the reason I never chose to be the driver when he was the passenger, because he was the king of backseat drivers.

Though ill and weak, he found the strength to transform himself into my personal driver education instructor. Many of his tips were helpful, but most of his comments were criticisms. His instruction never ended. Once I actually counted fourteen comments about my driving technique during one round-trip to Kaiser Hospital. Lots of trips to Kaiser, lots of "helpful" tips, lots of stress headaches.

I protested, "Enough already!" and put him on a ration of five criticisms during one round-trip, or I would find it necessary to make other arrangements for his transportation. My darling Denny tried so hard to accommodate me, but it wasn't easy for him to keep his mouth shut. Out of the corner of my eye, I would notice his hand fly up to issue directions to me, but he'd catch himself and pretend to adjust his cap or scratch his head. Or he might start to use a cautionary tone but substitute a fake little cough, or pretend that he forgot whatever it was he was going to say. And so it went, until he eventually returned to full-time monitoring of every mile I drove.

So, I tried the honest, up-front approach: "Honey, when I drive alone I have a lot of confidence, but when you're in the car I have none at all. My driving is growing worse, I'm anxious when you're my p-p-passenger [I started to cry right about here], and I dread these trips more than I can possibly tell you." The tears I shed were really big, and Denny felt terrible about it.

He felt so terrible that he began to compliment my driving. He praised my ability to stay in the middle of my own lane, my parking skills, and how confidently I passed slow cars. It felt like being patted on the head or patronized, so I never quite got out of my angry mode. I prayed a lot: "God, help Denny to get off my back, or help me to ignore him while I'm driving. I don't want to spend our precious time together being mad." We were in the car a lot; therefore, I prayed a lot!

Denny got sicker as his cancer spread, but he still had a mission concerning my driving. He managed to sneak in a comment or two, or three, or more, every trip to the hospital, and I grew accustomed to it after almost ten months of treatment. I had no idea what it was like to be in his body and what unexpressed feelings he might have had. Perhaps God had whispered to me in my dreams, "Betty, get used to it; he doesn't have much time left."

Indeed, he didn't. Aggressive treatment was hurting him more than helping and had to be discontinued. He was glad to be free of it. He was visibly thinner, weaker, and frailer than ever before. During his last week of life in our home, our family surrounded Denny and someone was always at his side. When he grew too weak to speak to us, he would smile and make a kiss with his lips or pat someone's arm. He died gently as we laid our hands on him and cried. It was an awesome experience. We were grateful that his struggle was over, but we were also numb with grief and exhaustion. The two weeks following Denny's death were a blur.

I remember a montage of signing papers, making arrangements for both a private and a public service, phone calls, housing out-of-state relatives, food appearing from nowhere, tears, hugging, and sharing memories.

Things had finally settled down a bit. The relatives were gone and so was the food. Thank-you notes were written; wonderful, supportive letters arrived each day filled with memories of Denny; and it felt good to cry. But it was quiet and lonely. I had so many things to do but I couldn't decide what to do first, so I did nothing each day.

One morning, I received a call from our representative at the memorial park nearby. "Mrs. Auchard, we have your husband's cremains ready for you." The container was small, wrapped neatly in brown paper, and presented to me in a dark green, velour drawstring bag. Very nice. Very respectful. I felt very tender toward this parcel as I hugged it to my chest, then set it in the seat beside me—the passenger seat. I gently patted it and even considered protecting it with a seat belt.

Then something occurred to me as I drove myself and this container home. This was probably the only time in our forty-nine years of life together that Denny was my passenger and wouldn't be saying a word about my driving. It struck me as humorous but sad. I caressed the velour bag again and wiped away my tears so I could see where I was going . . . 'cuz you gotta stay alert when you're driving.

Betty Auchard

*Few things are more rewarding than
a child's open, uncalculating devotion.*
VERA BRITTAIN

THINKING OF OTHERS,
SIX-YEAR-OLD-STYLE

My middle child, Jorey, is my sensitive daughter with all her highs and lows. She talks about and mourns her ancestors' deaths, though they may be from generations before her. She is the one who talks about God and heaven a lot. She believes that everyone in heaven rides horses, but it never hurts if they fall off as they fall onto the soft clouds. Jorey is the mothering older sister to all the younger children in her Montessori school on the company campus where I work. She greets each one by name and an accompanying hug as they pass her in the hallways at school. She thinks she'll be a mother, teacher, or doctor when she grows up.

This particular morning started out with the normal chaos that hits every weekday in my household of three children and one mommy. Jorey woke up on the wrong side of the bed from the moment her eyes fluttered open. She didn't want to get up, didn't want to get dressed, and was in tears when I told her that I hadn't been able to find her favorite granola bars at the grocery store the night before.

Oh, boy, here we go.

Jorey just needed me to hold her and help her get "started right." I did hold her for a few minutes, but as always we were running late. I couldn't hold her forever that day, so she just had to muddle through and get moving. I selfishly wished she would think of the rest of the family and how much it affects all of us when she acts like this in the morning. But I tried to quickly remind myself that she's a six-year-old child and not having her favorite granola bars is a big deal. We got out the door and into the van, Jorey in a bad mood along with an older brother and younger sister who were reacting to her foul disposition.

We dropped big brother off at his school, then headed to the girls' school before I was off to work. We arrived at the school and hung up the girls' coats. My daughter kneeled down to pull out something from her "cubby." She handed me a scroll, and I unrolled it. Jorey had written in pencil the following phonetic message:

> der Granpo dic and Granpo Cin
> Im sore Granmo Valma died,
> I'm shr you stil thenc ubawt the hape momins that you shard
> Love Jorey

My grandmother died earlier that year, and Jorey, on her own initiative, wrote a letter to Grandpa Dick and Great-Grandpa Ken. Choked up, I couldn't speak and could only put my arms around her to try to express what I was feeling.

Jorey is one of the most sensitive people I know; sometimes that is a challenge, but that is also one of the qualities that make her so special. She often thinks of others rather than herself. I will send her special scroll to Grandpa Dick and Great-Grandpa Ken and guess that, just as I did, they'll have tears in their eyes as they open it and read the brief but heartfelt message from their granddaughter and great-granddaughter.

The scroll may be made of white paper with pink construction paper hearts for decoration, but in my eyes it is made of pure gold, just like Jorey.

BRENDA GRANT

TAKING STOCK

I *awakened in the middle of the night with unbear-*
able leg pain. Eight hundred milligrams of Motrin later, I
still found no relief. When I dragged myself out of bed, I
winced in pain.

Gritting my teeth, I drove my two older children to school,
then, with my four-year-old son, Trent, in tow, I rushed to the office of a sports medicine chiropractor. He thought I might have a
hernia and sent me on to urgent care. In the emergency room I
found such comfort holding my son's small hand. His warmth
reassured me I could be strong, no matter what the outcome.

After hours of reading to my son, a doctor finally said, "I ordered a sonogram ASAP. You either have a hernia or, worst case,
an aneurysm."

"I don't have time for this," I said. "I need to pick up my kids
from school."

"Against my better judgment, I say pick your kids up and be
back here in thirty minutes."

I gathered my kids and told them to pray that our neighbor
would be home so I could get back to the hospital. When we arrived at her house, she pulled in behind me. She readily agreed to
keep the kids while I dashed back to the hospital.

The sonogram revealed my leg was fine. The doctor gave me
a "go home and rest" speech. Even though I knew lying in bed to
heal my leg was better than an operation, I still resented the torture of enforced inactivity.

Three days later, I received a call from my primary care physician. "I noticed you were in urgent care," he said. "I'm sorry to say they read your sonogram incorrectly. You need to come back in immediately and start treatment for a blood clot."

Here we go again, I thought while Trent and I scrambled out the door. In the car I prayed, "Lord, if I have to die, take me quickly. Help my kids hear Your voice clearly so they can manage any situation in life. Guide them, love them, and care for them."

At the doctor's office, a nurse ushered me in immediately. I gave Trent some toys, and the doctor, his face drawn and solemn, said, "This is very serious. You're a healthy, fit, thirty-six-year-old, and blood clots shouldn't be a problem. This is life-threatening—a little piece could break off, hit your lung, and you'd stop breathing. We'll give you two shots a day to help thin your blood. There's a risk of excessive bleeding, but it's the lesser of the two evils."

Just then the nurse peeked into the room. "Doctor, you've got that call you've been waiting for."

I glanced at my son playing, and surprisingly, peace penetrated my heart.

When the doctor came back, his eyes Ping-Ponged from ceiling to floor. "You're not going to believe this," he whispered. "It was a typo. You're fine. No blood clot. The clerk marked the wrong box on the summary sheet they sent my office. You can exercise all you want."

I leaped from the examining table and gave the doctor a big hug. I know God doesn't make mistakes. Somehow He has a plan in all of this. My leg's sore, but after this news, it doesn't feel too bad. Thank you, God!

The doctor looked embarrassed as he stuttered his apologies. I smiled and told him not to worry. I wasn't going to sue him for fifteen minutes of anxiety. I refused to waste another minute of my glorious new lease on life.

Minutes later, Trent and I swung hands to the car. On the way to pick up my two older children, I thought of the clutter that clogs my life. The daily schedule I struggle to complete: the piles of laundry, the empty fridge, the stack of dishes, even exercise. None of that seemed relevant anymore.

I count myself to be one of the privileged who has brushed close enough to the potential of death to take stock and find the essence of life. No matter what circumstance brings, faith, diligently serving my God; family, a little boy's precious hand; and friends who drop their agenda to help out at a moment's notice—faith, family, and friends—remain life's eternal constants. Everything else pales in comparison.

SUZY RYAN

II
TURNING UP YOUR LIGHT

One of the oldest human needs is having someone to wonder

where you are when you don't come home at night.

MARGARET MEAD

CIRCLE OF PLENTY

The learning prop our teacher used in a workshop I attended years ago was a one-dollar bill. Not just any dollar bill, though. The teacher called them "K" bills and said they were special because the mint distributed only a small batch of them. We were instructed to put the dollar away in a safe place until we felt an urge to spend it—all designed to teach us how to trust our intuition and validate our impulses. That's when I became compulsive about saving K bills and shared my ritual with others.

Although it was never my intention, I've been the recipient of others' impulses to spend their K bills. When I told my aunt about my K bill experience, she saved a batch and then gave them to me that year for my birthday. Now she deposits them in her granddaughter's investment account. And, ever since I shared my K bill story with my mom, she has been compulsive about saving them for me. But it hasn't stopped there.

My sister Pam, a mutual friend Elaine, and I were having lunch together one day. I remarked that the food was just as great as the last time we'd all been at the restaurant. When Elaine responded that she'd never been there before, Pam and I insisted that she had—with us. Elaine countered again. We persisted. I even pointed out the booth we'd been in and described what each of us had for dinner. Because I had no doubt, suddenly an impulse possessed me.

"I'll bet you a hundred dollars that I'm right," I said.

Before I could retract it, Elaine said, "You're on."

Throughout lunch, Pam and I puzzled over Elaine's forgetful-ness. She was acting out of character. As a rule, she's reliably right. Was our friend losing it? While Elaine was away from the table, Pam and I questioned why the three of us would have gathered there the last time so that we could help Elaine remem-ber. Instead, we identified an event that involved a different per-son, not Elaine after all! Rather than disclosing this lapse of memory to her, my sister and I agreed that we wouldn't give Elaine the satisfaction of being right too quickly.

By then, I was fretting about paying the bet. How was I going to come up with $100 on my student income? Then I remembered my K bill savings ritual. This was a perfect solution for amassing $100.

One by one, I began to hide what K bills I had in the bed-and-breakfast Elaine owns. With the help of an accomplice, the bills were secretly placed inside a decorative gourd on the tallest of her kitchen shelves. Many months went by. Finally, the hundredth K bill was saved and hidden. In the meantime, neither Pam nor I mentioned the bet to Elaine again. And as though she'd forgotten about it, she never called me on it, either.

I couldn't wait to present the K bills in person, so I called Elaine up one morning in the middle of her breakfast serving. I told her to get a ladder and take down the gourd. Elaine loves surprises, so she was extremely cooperative in spite of her B-and-B duties.

When Elaine opened the lid and saw the contents, she let out a screech. While I reminded her of the bet and confessed my mistake, she poured the bills out all over her buffet counter. I shared with her how I saved the money and explained that it was hers for the spending on one condition: she had to take me with her so I could watch her spend them. "Absolutely," Elaine said. As I hung up the phone, I could hear her laughing while laying out the story to her bed-and-breakfast guests. The next week she visited and treated me to a great lunch and movie with her K for-tune, but she still had a wad left when she headed home.

Unbeknownst to me, Elaine had no intention of accepting the payment. Instead, she went to Pam's gift shop, dumped the remaining K bills on the sales counter, and said, "I want to buy some of your seashells; you know, the pretty ones I've been wanting for my conversation table. And let's figure a way to get the rest of the money back to your sister."

Pam didn't have a problem coming up with a plan, having already channeled K bills to me on the sly. Without my knowing, Pam had been routing some my way ever since I told her how I was going to pay back the bet. Now, that may seem like the bet was at Pam's expense, but here's where the plot thickens and the give-and-take gets more complex.

Since my mother has been compelled to save K bills for me from long ago, whenever she helps out at my sister's gift shop, she inspects the cash drawer for any of the uncommon K bills. While I was saving up the bet money, any K bills that crossed Pam's path were planted in the till for Mom to "discover." After the bet was paid and some of those familiar K bills were back in my sister's hands, into the cash drawer they went, a few at a time. Mom unwittingly completed the circle of plenty by trading for them and passing them on to me. When all this was revealed to Mom, she was only too pleased to be part of this game of reciprocity.

The gourd container is now a cherished artifact. Like a "horn of plenty," it is our token of fullness. With its classic womblike shape, it suggests nurturing and exudes abundance just like my circle of compassionate and reciprocating female kin.

DEBBIE PETRICEK

I think the one lesson I have learned
is that there is no substitute for paying attention.
DIANE SAWYER

DOING THE HOKEY POKEY

I waved goodbye to my parents on the day after my nine-year-old daughter's birthday. The house was a wreck. I was exhausted. All I wanted to do was curl up on the couch now that the weekend was officially winding down, but the adult in me had to gear up to finish reports for the next day's meetings. And the mother in me had to convince Meredith to do the final push on her six-week-long class project.

I took a deep breath and found her examining the "Make Your Own Scent" kit I had given to her. "Honey, we don't have time to play!"

"Please, Mom. I'm almost finished with my Alaska project. Can't we try this first?" She looked up at me with big brown eyes; tiny freckles scattered across her nose.

It is her birthday weekend, and she has been a good sport about the other weekend obligations that left little time for playing with her gifts. "Okay," I said. *How long can it take anyway?*

"Yes!" she cheered, and tore into the box, dumping two vials, a glass jar, a cork, a coiled copper tube, and instructions onto the floor. "The book says to use fresh flower petals," she said as I looked over her shoulder at the suggested list of good perfume-making ingredients. "We need ethyl alcohol," she read, "and ani-mal fat, such as ordinary lard, for the enfleurage step where aro-matic oils are absorbed from the flowers."

"Enfleurage? Aromatic oils?" I winced. "And lard? We'll have to go to the store to get *that*."

Within the hour, a half cup of lard was melting in the jar in a pan of hot water. "No stems," Meredith warned as we plucked petals from her birthday bouquet. Next, we poured the liquid fat into the jar, filled the remainder with petals, and shoved the cork into the top.

"Shake it," I said, reading the instructions. "Then we wait for an hour, shaking the bottle at intervals." Meredith shook the jar and placed it on the kitchen counter. I set the timer for ten minutes.

No sooner had I sat down at the computer than the mi-crowave beeped. Excited, Meredith grabbed my hand. "It's time to shake!" I sighed and followed her to the kitchen. She gripped the jar and burst out singing, "Put your right foot in—Mom!" I laughed and followed her lead. "You put your right foot out . . . then you shake it all about. You do the Hokey Pokey and you turn yourself around." She giggled. "That's what it's all about. Hokey Pokey!"

During the hour, we danced the Hokey Pokey five times.

Next, we placed the soggy petals in a colander to drain the fat, but no liquid seeped through. "Squeeze 'em," Meredith in-structed, "but don't let them go down the drain!" Immediately, repulsive yellow "fat-and-petal-essence" oozed through my fin-gers into the jar.

Finally, Meredith poured alcohol into the concoction, shoved the cork in, shook it all around, and placed the jar in a pan of water on the stove. I inserted one end of the copper tube into the cork and the other into the vial on the counter, securing it with the condenser support.

After turning on the heat to begin the distillation, I tried to work, but every five minutes Meredith said, "Let's check it."

Each time, I muttered, "Nothing's happening," and adjusted the temperature.

Meredith curled up to read about Alaska's famous people, and I focused on my report until a deafening blast rattled the windows.

Meredith shot up from her seat. "What was *that*?" she cried, and dashed after me to the kitchen.

"Oh no!" We stepped over apparatus strewn across the floor. Overhead, yellow blobs riddled the ceiling. Scorched metal permeated the air as the empty jar sizzled against the bottom of the red-hot pan. "Move back in case the jar explodes!" I shrieked, grabbing the pot and plunging it into the sink.

Meredith watched as I knelt down to pick up the vial and sniffed it. "I don't believe this," I moaned, and waved the bottle under her nose. "There's no smell."

We stared at the bottle, dumbfounded.

"That's okay, Mom." Meredith wrapped her arms around me, pressing a kiss hard against my cheek. We tumbled backward against the floor. "It was fun anyway." She giggled as we stared at the messy ceiling.

"Fun? *Fun*?" I mocked, laughing in spite of myself. "Next time I'd rather *eat* the lard!"

"I love you, Mom," Meredith proclaimed with a mixture of affection and gratitude.

"You too," I murmured, delighted that our afternoon together had put that shine in her eyes.

The next morning when driving to work, a sign caught my eye: PARENTS, CHILDREN NEED YOUR PRESENCE, NOT YOUR PRESENTS. "No kidding," I said aloud. I hummed the rest of the way, eventually belting out, "And that's what it's all about. Hokey Pokey!"

DEBRA AYERS BROWN

CAVIAR AND MOONSHINE

I *am being wooed by a very eccentric man living two* hours south of me in New York City. Two hours may not seem like a lot, but it is the difference between Manhattan and a very small town in the remote backwoods of northeastern Pennsylvania beside the very beautiful Delaware River. My house is nestled into hundreds of wooded acres, a short hike up from the river among the critters who laid claim to this little corner of paradise long before I discovered it. My closest neighbors are about half a mile up at the top of the hill. Mr. and Mrs. Quinn have looked out for me since I moved here about five years ago. Mrs. Quinn is getting on in age. She keeps an eagle eye out for any passersby as she crochets by her big picture window.

I was born and bred in an equally small town in Georgia, grew up, moved to Manhattan, only to escape back into the woods, building myself a house square in the middle of nowhere. A friend once told me that no one but a Southerner would build a house so far off the main road, and he was right. Being a Southerner, I wasn't familiar enough with the endless Northern winters to realize that my long, gradually graded driveway had to be repeatedly plowed. Nor had I realized that a four-wheel-drive vehicle would be necessary to accomplish any sort of delivery. Emissaries from the post office, UPS, FedEx, or the local florist all risk entrapment at the bottom of the driveway. Consequently, Mrs. Quinn accepts offerings from all wayward, nonequipped vehicles bringing me essentials from the outside world.

In this process of being wooed, I began to receive parcels. The first to arrive was a little box from FedEx in mid-February. Because surprise packages delight Mrs. Quinn as much as they do me, I ripped into my Express Overnight delivery as soon as she handed it over. We were both very astonished to discover that it was a tin of Beluga caviar on dry ice and a sweet note wishing me a "Happy Valentine's Day." Having no particular fondness for fish eggs, I brought the tin home, stuck it in my refrigerator, and got a lot of mileage out of talking about the most unusual Valentine I had ever received.

This area where I've chosen to locate tends to collect odd and unusual people, which is probably why I feel at home. My friend Karen, a wonderfully adventurous cook, suggested that I make sushi with the caviar. The idea had merit until I discussed it with another friend, Lynn. She nearly went into cardiac arrest at the thought of Beluga being so debased. Lynn has a wealth of information about things esoteric and obscure. She's lived an amazing life: finding herself in unknown corners of the world, participating in wild tribal rituals, and eating foods most of us would never think of consuming. So, it wasn't surprising to find out that Lynn is a caviar maven. She suggested a "caviar party."

Prolonged feelings of isolation coupled with the overwhelming color of white had worn me slick after long months of endless winter. Being a Southerner, I am constitutionally unprepared for cold weather and suffer bouts of Seasonal Affective Disorder due to insufficient sunlight. (I diagnosed that one myself.) In March, I was still shoveling snow while my sister and her family in Florida had already gone through an entire bottle of sunscreen.

Bronson, my fourteen-year-old, already tan nephew, flew up from Florida to visit his seasonally challenged aunt—and to see snow for the first time. So, with an occasion to celebrate, the party began to take shape. As luck would have it, Mrs. Quinn's fourteen-year-old granddaughter and her family are my next closest neighbors. I invited them so Bronson would have a "babe" his own age to hang with.

Lynn was responsible for all the caviar accoutrements. She informed me that if we were going to do this thing correctly, we should also serve chilled vodka. That made me think of a local legend by the name of "Tater Bug." One of Tater Bug's great gifts is his ability to make high-quality moonshine. This being the backwoods, we decided to forgo Absolut in favor of honest-to-God, 190 proof home brew—chilled, of course.

My great good friends Alan and Bill were up for the weekend from the city. As it is our habit to eat at least one meal together during their visits, I invited them over for the big event. Both are pianists, singers, and/or voice teachers in New York and Europe. In total, ten of us—all with four-wheel-drive vehicles, all feeling worn from the length of the season—congregated for the decanting of the Beluga.

Lynn was the official in charge. She showed us how to delicately slather toast points with rare fish roe, finely chopped eggs and onions, and spritz them with lemon. The first reviews were tentative. Bronson thought it tasted a little like oysters a bit past their prime. Emma, his babe, thought it was too salty. She much preferred eating the toast point sans caviar. Lynn swore that Arnold's Brick Oven White was the bread of choice for the former Iranian ambassador's caviar, and she would be the one person in the world to have personal knowledge of such. We sipped Tater Bug's chilled moonshine from martini glasses, had our fill of caviar, and caught up on the details of each others' lives. It was indeed a radical thing we did, staving off the monotony of winter by getting together to celebrate backwoods community with caviar.

Now, I am cosmopolitan enough to know that spaghetti dinners do not regularly follow Beluga. But this is the backwoods, and we are a collection of the odd and unusual, so we took a culinary leap of faith. Our palates seemed none the worse for wear after following Beluga and moonshine with spaghetti and more moonshine. Dinner conversation included a short course in high school chemistry as Tater Bug explained exactly what takes place in the distillation process. Lynn revealed a little of how she came to have such a great love for, and familiarity with, caviar and how she knew so much about the Shah of Iran's caviar preferences. We all laughed a lot.

Emma's older sister, Melanie, sang "Amarilli, Mia Bella," opera style, accompanied by Bill (without music) on my newly refurbished old piano. Standing there in her jeans and white T-shirt, her voice and her persona were a paradox of youthful sweetness and womanly potential. We prevailed upon Alan to sing, and then Bill.

He sat down at the piano, without fanfare, and sang a mythic fable song about a king, a maiden, and a meadowlark who lost its voice and its life. In the end I could not decide if I was wiping tears from my eyes because of the beauty of the song, the delicate perfection of movement as his fingers effortlessly traversed the entire keyboard, the pure place that was the source of his voice—or because all of this was taking place in my home in the middle of nowhere, in the middle of an otherwise cold, ordinary winter night. Everyone there contributed in some special way.

It seems like a miracle that my being wooed would lead to such a perfect thing as our backwoods caviar-and-moonshine party—without the wooer even in attendance. We toasted our absent, eccentric New Yorker for giving us all something exquisitely rare, something far greater than a Valentine tin of Beluga. He gave us a jump-start, an excuse to gather and strengthen our bonds to each other and to the collection of the odd and unusual we steadfastly claim as our community: a neighbor who looks out for you, a legendary distiller of bootleg spirits, a caviar maven, two concert pianists, an aspiring opera singer, and a four-teen-year-old fan of white bread toast points.

Despite snow, isolation, and Seasonal Affective Disorder, we all gathered to sample the exotic and ended up recognizing and celebrating that same quality in each other and ourselves. This ordinary winter night simply could not have been any more splendid.

MYRA WINNER

PENNIES FROM HEAVEN

"*Life isn't fair.*" I first remember hearing those words coming from my dad when I was only eight years old. He had asked me to take my sister's hairbrush upstairs. I protested—but he prevailed. My brothers and sister and I jokingly kept that phrase alive throughout our growing-up years.

Even though "life isn't fair," Dad always had a way of making each one of us feel like his favorite child. Carol, my older sister, remembers him saying to her, "You're Daddy's girl, and I'll always take care of you." My twin brother, Kent, and I had just arrived on the scene, and she felt threatened.

Before Dad died two years ago, he designated Kent as the executor of his estate. Kent's wife called me out of concern about how she thought things were shaking out with Dad's will. I was concerned, too, about fairness and equity. After all, when there's nothing else to give, love equals money. Or so I thought.

When his will was read, Dad had specified that the majority of his assets go to Kent and his wife, with most of the remaining portion split equally between five remaining siblings—his original family and his stepfamily.

I couldn't understand Dad's rationale for the unequal distribution. Did he love Kent more? Did he love me less? My hurt and anger became like an emotional cancer eating away at my internal well-being. I wanted to release the pain, but I didn't know how. On one level, I knew Dad loved me. In fact, he adored me and was proud of my accomplishments. But he also chose to dis-tribute his estate in a way that made no sense to me. How could he be so unfair?

As I slogged through my feelings of anger, hurt, and betrayal for over a year, I didn't like who I'd become. I wanted a new tape to play in my head—one that wasn't constantly sorting through the "whys." As long as I focused on the inequity, I continued to miss the many blessings that seemed to be erased from my memory of Dad. I needed to find the sweetness in all this mess with my dad. But sweetness comes with time.

A year after Dad died, my heart opened wide one morning as I sat quietly in an easy chair in my office. "Amazing Grace" played softly in the background—the same music played at Dad's funeral. My eyes stopped at one of the treasures on my private altar—a tiny gold pillow inscribed with the message LET IT GO. I kept saying those words over and over as I let the phrase sink in. And just before I closed my eyes to meditate, I noticed Amigo— our white fluffy Himalayan cat—lounging in total contentment on the ottoman in front of me. Just the kind of peace I was seeking. The silence of the moment became a revelation.

Precious memories began to appear and reappear as I reflected on all of the wonderful gifts that Dad gave to me during our time together. I saw Dad as the rock of my existence for so long. I remembered him lovingly reading stories to us all at bedtime and how he helped me with my homework. I remembered how he patiently taught me to drive a stick shift and how he became my personal golf coach as I learned the game. I remember how he got us all through the unexpected, heartbreaking death of our mother when I was fifteen. I remembered him teaching me to cook. I remembered how much he laughed and how little he complained. I reminisced on how strict Dad was with me when I started dating boys, and how lenient he was with my twin brother when he dated girls. Even then, it wasn't always fair, but we had fun and somehow it made sense and even felt good to be so loved and protected.

More insights flowed as I "let go" and let God deal with the stuff troubling me. Ironically, it took my anguishing over not getting what I felt was my "share" of Dad to discover all that he'd already given me. The biggest gift being his unconditional love throughout my life. That love left me free to take on the world without any childhood baggage to lug along with me.

I could feel the presence of Spirit deepening within me as I continued to let go. The anger and pain began to be replaced by thanksgiving and grace. From this place, I could count my blessings. I rediscovered that everyone did the best they knew how at the time—and that life isn't always fair. That's all. I had just journeyed into "graceland," where only love and compassion reside.

"Your light shines brightly from up here," Dad whispered in my ear, still loving and protecting me in his own unique way, "and I'll be sending you pennies from heaven."

KAY ALLENBAUGH

A SECOND CHANCE

*O*ur son, Erik, has always preferred quiet birthdays: "Could I just have a friend over and maybe we
could all go out to dinner?" His simple desires made
birthdays fun and easy. There was one birthday, however, that
none of us will ever forget. He was twenty-four that year.

Erik came to live with us when he was two and a half months
old. His birth mother was fifteen, the birth father just one year
older. They were still in school. "Usually a child is placed for
adoption right away," the caseworker apologized, "but in this
case, the families had an unusually difficult time releasing their
precious little boy." We could certainly understand.

Once he was placed in our arms, no power on earth could
have removed him. We loved him irreversibly from that first moment. My husband and I believed that love alone could have em-
powered the birth families to make the decision to let him go.
They wanted him to have a chance to grow up in a family prepared for him. I cried because of their pain.

As the months passed, my thoughts turned less and less to
Erik's birth family. Oh, there were special times when I'd think of
them, like on his birthday and at Christmas. Sometimes I just
wished that I could tell them I was sorry they were missing all
the joy he brought to our lives every day. I wanted to say, "Thank
you for giving us so much happiness."

Erik and my husband were the "mighty twosome," always
together. They loved anything active: a sports event for every
season. It was clear by the first grade that Erik was a talented ath-

lete. A gift inherited from his birth father, encouraged and developed by his adopted father.

By high school graduation, Erik had traded his interest in sports for interest in one special girl. They were the new "mighty twosome" in our home. Plans for a June wedding that would be on the seventh anniversary of their first date together was announced. Since I was a minister, they asked me to perform the ceremony. I was thrilled! But the most thrilling announcement came just four months later.

Erik and Karen were expecting their first child. He was quiet when they dropped by to give us the good news. Happily his bride and I squealed and danced around in a circle. For the next few minutes everybody seem to talk at once. "Mom, Dad, would you be hurt if we tried to locate my birth parents?" Erik finally said. "We just have so many questions, and with the baby coming . . ." His voice trailed off.

"We understand," my husband and I replied almost in unison. "We'll help in the search. But first, can we all agree that if the birth parents are found we'll protect their privacy?"

"Yes," Erik said. "I don't even know if I want to meet them." A letter to Children's Services for a volunteer adoption registry yielded nothing. Contact with adoption support groups was nonproductive. Months passed.

In the excitement of the birth of their baby boy, Kaleb, the adoption search was almost abandoned. But still, we couldn't let it go. Small pieces of seemingly insignificant information swirled in my head. Suddenly, like a puzzle, all the pieces seemed to fit together and the next step in our search was clear. The name of the birth father was secured. A letter was written to him and delivered in private by a trusted friend. He requested a meeting with my husband and me without Erik present.

How could we go through with this? What would we uncover? Our nerves were on edge as we drove to the scheduled meeting place. *Will life ever be the same after this day?* we wondered. When our son's father walked through the door, we shook hands and then hugged. "Thank you," we whispered to each other, our voices choked with tears.

Later we talked in turn, each telling a personal story. We presented him with pictures of Erik growing up in our family. "I was adopted, too," he said. "Before Erik meets me, if he decides to, I want him to know that. Also, tell him I discovered who my birth parents were, they being close friends of my adopted parents, when I was thirteen. Tell him my wife and four children know about him. Everyone will be glad to meet him someday if he wants. But it's okay if he doesn't. He should think about it and be sure." Just before we said goodbye he said, "And, one more thing, please continue to search for his mother. I saw her twelve years ago. She has never gotten over giving him up." We promised to continue the search. It would be easier now.

In less than two weeks, I heard her voice on the telephone.

"Hello."

"You and I have never met, but we have something wonderful in common."

"Tell me what," she said with excitement.

"Can you talk privately?" I asked.

"Yes!" she said in a loud whisper.

"I am the mother who adopted your baby boy."

"I prayed to God this day would come," she cried. "I told my boys someday their older brother would walk in our door. And now he will. Oh, thank you, thank you."

"I'm the one who is grateful," I said through tears.

"When can I see him?" she asked.

We agreed to come to her home the following week.

It was with mixed emotions that we arrived on that early September day. Children and dogs came out to greet us. She trailed behind. Anyone could see that she and Erik were mother and son by their hair color, eyes, smiles, and even mannerisms. I had not expected that! She invited us to come inside. As we passed through the kitchen, I noticed a freshly baked and frosted cake on the counter.

In the living room, we presented her with a framed picture collage of Erik's growing-up years and his wedding. She could not take her eyes off his face. Occasionally she reached out to touch him. Her five-year-old son continually interrupted, "Mommy, cut the cake, cut the cake." Finally she agreed and went alone into the kitchen. While others talked, I stepped to the kitchen door. I could see the lines of emotion in her face as she lowered the knife to cut the first piece of cake. And then it struck me!

"This is a birthday cake," I said. "You baked it because you can finally celebrate your son's birth."

"How did you know?" She gasped and began to sob.

I took her in my arms and said, "Mothers just know these things."

CLARA OLSON

It is the friends you can call up
at 4 A.M. that matter.
MARLENE DIETRICH

THE GATHERING

The Wild Women is what we call ourselves. We may not run with the wolves exactly, but in our salad days we came darn close. Most of us are well over forty and in our prime. We are a motley crew. All of us have been divorced (some more than once), some are married for the third time, and some, such as I, have been single for many years. All but one of us have children; all but one of us are teachers. We juggle family and career like the plate spinners on the old *Ed Sullivan Show*. We even remember the *Ed Sullivan Show*. We wear our years like a red badge of courage—and some of us even admit our age.

Once a quarter we gather to bare our souls. There are always at least six of us, and on a few occasions there have been as many as a dozen when students who have become our friends pass through our college classes to other voices, other rooms. But a true Wild Woman gathering consists of a handful of women crowded around a kitchen table where for the entirety of an evening we gorge on a veritable cornucopia of gustatory delights: platters of buffalo wings, hot and spicy and dripping with fat; towers of guacamole; bowls of garlicky salsa; mountains of greasy corn chips; a jug of wine; a pitcher of margaritas; and the requisite plate of fruit.

The preliminary conversation is unpretentious. We exchange pleasantries, catch up on the news, chat about academic matters, and compliment one another lavishly. "You've lost weight!" we exclaim as we stuff corn chips sagging with guacamole into our lying mouths. No one praises the cook. There is no cook at the gathering. Martha Stewart is banished to her organic garden. KFC and Sam's rule. Occasionally one of us will lapse into a pre–Wild Woman consciousness and appear at the door with a Tupperware bowl full of homemade cheese straws that we fall upon with the rapacity of piranhas. But the true allure of a Wild Woman evening is take-out, disposable plates, and the prospect of a languorous evening replete with lively conversation, intimate disclosures, and the fun of feeling seventeen again.

We arrive each lugging an overnight bag and favorite pillow. We may forget our hairbrushes, but we never forget our pills. Gaily colored dispensers loaded with Premarin, therapeutic vitamins, and St. John's wort line the bathroom counter, flanked by contact lens cases and the obligatory toothbrushes. When we leave in the morning wearing yesterday's makeup, we look more like raccoons in rumpled pajamas than like wolves.

We come for carrion comfort and we feast on it all evening. At length the conversation reaches the topic we have all been waiting for—the hard copy version of our private lives. All else is prologue. Those of us who are single envy those who are married. Not because we have any desire to be married but because we envy their intimacy with the opposite sex. Ordinary and predictable though it may be, it is more than we unattached denizens can dream of in this age of AIDS and ax murderers.

We have been partners in this dance for over twenty years. We are not easily shocked. In a good evening there may be one or two eyebrow-raising revelations, but these moments are as rare as they are titillating. For the most part we, too, are predictable.

We are as comfortable with each other as in a well-worn marriage. We know we are accepted. We know who we are. We are mothers, lovers, scholars, and friends, but—for one brief and fragile moment—we are wild!

PENNE J. LAUBENTHAL

OUT OF DARKNESS

*E*ver since I was a child, I have been afraid of the dark. At bedtime, I read until I got sleepy enough to doze off, letting the book fall on my chest and the bedroom light stay on. When my mother called for me to turn off the light, I opened the curtains so the bright street lamp lit the room. I left doors open and hall lights on. Without my book and my light, the few minutes of dark with only my thoughts terrified me.

Diane changed all that.

Diane was not even fifty when she was diagnosed with colon cancer. I first met her when she came to our cancer survivors support group frightened and in tears. Her prognosis was very serious; the cancer was widespread and the doctors did not give her long to live.

I belonged to the group because I was recovering from my second colon cancer. "I'm making it, Diane," I told her, "and so will you." I told her about my mother, who had been expected to die of colon cancer and was still alive forty-five years later. Still, I worried that I was raising her hopes in vain. Her chances were so slim. Was I being fair or honest?

As the weeks passed, Diane's panic turned to acceptance, her fear to a deep serenity that helped us all. Although she still cried easily, she also developed a sly, quiet sense of humor. It was hard to feel sorry for yourself when Diane was there to give your self-pity a sharp stab of her wit.

In the summer she began an experimental treatment, carrying

an automatic pump full of chemotherapy drugs in a fanny pack so she could have treatment around the clock. She could no longer drive, and friends shared the weekly drive to the research center in Buffalo with her.

"If we leave a half hour early," she'd tell them, "we could stop at my favorite bakery on the way. They have the most delicious blueberry muffins."

By fall, she was struggling with the heavy doses of chemotherapy. By then, the cancer had spread to her brain.

She made careful plans for her teenage son, finding a family who would care for him and a second friend who would back them up.

She and I daydreamed about her returning to her second-graders in January, although we both knew the possibility of her being able to go back was very small. "Maybe I can go in and read to them," she said. "They'd like that." She put off accepting permanent disability and told the school district that she wanted to keep her options open.

She had taught in the same elementary school for over twenty years. In warm weather, she always took the children outdoors and read to them under the trees. She was loved and respected by a whole generation of children she had taught and by their families.

Diane had made her peace with dying but was most frightened of being alone in the hospital when the time came. A group of us took turns being with her overnight, and that is how I learned not to be afraid of the dark.

I arrived at the hospital late one evening, paperback novel in hand, to take over staying with Diane from one of her teacher friends. Diane's untouched dinner tray was still in a corner of the room. I dribbled a little bit of water from a straw onto her cracked, dry lips, and she patted my hand.

The nurses had brought a recliner into the room for the people who were spending nights with Diane. I settled into it with a blanket over my legs. We sat for a long time, talking a bit, but mostly just being quiet. Finally, Diane seemed asleep, so I picked up my book.

Her eyes popped open. "Time for you to go to sleep," she said, and snapped off the light.

The room was very dark. There was not even a light from the parking lot outside; the door to the hall was closed. I heard Diane snoring softly in the big hospital bed, and I fell quietly asleep in the deep darkness, my book unopened.

I slept soundly, stretched out in that big chair, for several hours until the lights went on with a sudden blaze, and I woke up to the clatter of nurses helping Diane get out of bed.

Diane was no longer able to get up a few days later when she beckoned me close to her, kissed my cheek, and said goodbye. She died three days later, with a friend nearby.

I still read in bed at night, but now when I begin to get sleepy, I reach over and turn off the light. Oftentimes, I think of Diane. I see the twinkle in her eye, I smell blueberry muffins, and I re-member the stories of her vacation to the ocean, picture her reading to the children sitting under the trees. Then I go to sleep, so grateful for another day.

KATE MURPHY

GIVING IT AWAY

I lost a promotion and became depressed.
I gave my spirit away—
   to a Job.

I was hurt and disappointed by a friend,
and found myself angry overlong.
I gave my spirit away—
   to Another Person.

I didn't get my dream right away,
so I stopped trying.
I gave my spirit away—
   to my Lack of Patience.

I felt the rain upon my winter door,
and complained for lack of sun.
I gave my spirit away—
   to the Weather.

I looked upon the things I had
and called them not enough.
I gave my spirit away—
   to Feelings of Lack.

I ran myself ragged
and lost my sense of peace.

I gave my spirit away—
     to Time and Deeds.

I saw a challenge as a problem,
and feared the worst would happen.
I gave my spirit away—
     to Worry.

I competed with my neighbor's money
and success, and my ego suffered with defeat.
I gave my spirit away—
     to an image based on Things.

I lived my life alone sometimes
with nary a help from God nor angels nor men,
then felt the loneliness at that day's end.
I gave my spirit away—
     to Walls I did not love.

And as time progressed, I thought
I was missing something, and I was . . .
for I had given away—
     the very spirit that was Me!

So in counting my blessings this year,
I listed my own spirit
     as something I held dear.

And then set forth to nurture it—
to find my inner stillness
     within the claims that each day made.

To make decisions both large and small,
from a different kind of place,

from the wise center of my heart—
  where spirit lives.

And when I did so, when I honored it,
instead of the ego I knew so well,
my spirit grew in peace and strength—
for I was no longer
  giving it away.

SHEILA STEPHENS

III
OUR FAVORITE
FURRY ONES

*I believe that animals have been talking to human
beings ever since we were all made and put into this world.*

BARBARA WOODHOUSE

May all the dogs that I have ever loved
carry my coffin,
howl at the moonless sky,
and lie down with me sleeping
when I die.
ERICA JONG

MY GUIDING LIGHT

At age thirty-four, *I found that my life was shaping up in a really nice way.* I had a good job as a pediatric nurse, a happy marriage, an African Gray parrot named Sterling whose vocabulary was growing daily, my pilot's license, and a knack for making intricate jewelry.

That was twelve years ago, about the time I came home one night after my shift at the hospital and squirted some over-the-counter drops into my tired eyes. Instantly, I knew something was horribly wrong. I couldn't see, and the pain in my eyes was excruciating. I ended up being a random victim of tampering. Some never-to-be-found stranger had put lye in the eyedrops I bought.

I spent a good portion of the next four months lying in bed struggling with the shock of it all—my despair, anger, depression, and fear with being permanently blind. I wanted to die. I couldn't imagine my life without sight, and in my mind, I focused on all the things I could no longer do. I wanted my independence back. So much had changed. I felt like a small child dependent on others, learning all over again how to tie my shoes, match my clothes, cook without hurting myself, and go outside. Over and over I wondered, *If I can't see and have to rely on others, how will there ever be meaning in my life?*

My husband wanted things to be the same when they weren't, and eventually we divorced. My mother—who was devastated—felt that she had to protect me, and a number of friends felt awkward in my presence now that I was blind. Ultimately, it was my concern for everyone else that finally pushed me up and out into finding a way to be in my tenuous new world.

Using a cane was when I felt the most blind. I could literally feel people shying away from me when I walked—maybe they feared my condition was contagious. I couldn't count all my bruises from bumping into tree branches and stumbling on cracks in the sidewalk and stairs and curbs.

The day I got my first guide dog—Webster—is the day my life took a positive turn. Webbie took me through the biggest transitions of all, but due to an unforeseen and unusual medical condition, Webster had to "retire" after four years of work. Yet he facilitated my having a life like everyone else, and a piece of my heart went with him.

Deanne, my beautiful, statuesque German shepherd, has been at my side for years now, and I wish I could freeze-frame her at this age. With each year together, our relationship has deepened and her work gets better. Guide dogs tend to average eight years of service, and already I can't imagine being without her.

Deanne, my guiding light, sees for me and assists me safely down streets, through crosswalks, up stairs, into stores and schools, into cars, and onto airplanes. In spite of all her good work, I love her the most when she snuggles next to me in bed. Once I'm asleep, she jumps down onto the floor to rest, anxious for a new day. But when I'm traveling and staying in a hotel,

Deanne instinctively knows to lie on top of the bed, sleeping near me all night long.

In my search for independence, I went back to the hospital where I'd worked to try a different job, transcribing medical reports. Although I didn't find the work as stimulating as I'd hoped, all was not lost. That's where I met my new husband. His ability to see me as I am comes from his experience with his brother, who has multiple sclerosis. My husband witnessed up close how people in general treat someone differently who has a handicap. He knew his brother had not changed on the inside, and he knows I haven't, either. One of his favorite things to do is read to me. I love his deep, soothing voice and his gift of describing things in a way that I can see.

My life is once again shaping up in a really nice way. I have moved on to a new job that I dearly love. I'm the director of volunteers for Guide Dogs for the Blind. I travel, do public speaking, recruit volunteers, and give lots of tours of the expansive guide-dog campus in northern California—Deanne leading the way. And I frequently fly to the Oregon campus for graduation ceremonies, with my sweet shepherd nestled comfortably at my feet.

A special thing I get to do is visit grade schools and talk with children about guide dogs and being blind. After we spend time together, they learn what I now know—being blind doesn't have to be scary, it's just different. To put everyone at ease when Deanne and I enter a classroom, I begin by telling the students that we all have five senses. We then practice using them. I may have the kids tie their shoes with their eyes closed so that they can think like I do.

Now that I focus on all the things I *can* do, I say to the children, "There are only two things I can't do now that I'm blind. What do you think they are?" A flurry of hands go up as they guess the two things. I usually answer driving a car and flying a plane. Then I explain that one of the few times Deanne and I are apart is when I feed my adventurous spirit by rowing in a racing scull in the exciting, turbulent San Francisco Bay. My buddies join me, and they row nearby.

Recently I got to see how far I'd come in my journey to independence. I gave a guide-dog campus tour for a group of blind children, all of whom used canes. Many of them were terrified of the big dogs, so to begin with we went to the kennels. There the children could pet and cuddle 150 irresistible puppies in training. They let the pups lick their cheeks, and they ran their fingers over the dogs' fur to learn how to tell a German shepherd from a lab. By the end of the tour, many children knew they, too, wanted to have a guide dog someday.

I have several nicknames for my beloved Deanne, including Doodlebug, Pooh Bear, and D.D. And Sterling knows every one of them. When my husband, Deanne, and I get ready for bed, we typically hear "Good night, D.D." or "Good dog," mimicked to sound like me just after we cover Sterling's cage.

It's been twelve years now since I've seen my reflection in a mirror. But if I could, I already know what I'd see—thanks to Deanne. I'd see a confident, fulfilled, independent woman who has created a "new normal" for herself and has found richness in her very meaningful life.

AERIAL GILBERT

FRISKY

Candy was still a meticulously groomed brown-and-black stuffed dog when, after twenty-five years, I gave her to my son. As well she should have been, since she had spent the majority of her life snoozing on my bed. Santa brought Candy to me when I was in the third grade. When Kenny reached that same age, I passed ownership of Candy on to him.

Immediately, Kenny changed the name and sex of his new pet, as only little boys can do. What boy would admit to owning a female pet named Candy? Now known as Frisky, he followed Kenny everywhere during the day, and they slept together every night. Kenny's dreams were no doubt sweeter and his bed more comfortable because Frisky was there. Kenny loved Frisky. In fact, Kenny loved Frisky until Frisky was limp from the hugs and furless from the petting.

Kenny, Frisky, and I once took a never-to-be-forgotten trip with Kenny's grandparents. Kenny's granddaddy was at the wheel as we headed for a relative's house in Roanoke, Alabama. Right before arriving, we stopped at a drugstore in Roanoke to purchase a few things. In the midst of it all, somehow Frisky was left on a bottom shelf in the store. Kenny didn't miss Frisky until we were about twenty-five miles farther down the road. He immediately began imploring his granddaddy to go back, but Kenny's grandfather, being the always practical, time-conscious, no-nonsense type, could see no reason to upset the schedule and return for such a scruffy pup. However, he did eventually surrender to our pleas when he realized he would get no peace, and probably no forgiveness, from us or from Grandmother until he did.

All the way back I chewed my nails and wondered, *What if he's not there?* Grandmother was obviously worrying in her own way. She could never bear to see her "grandbaby" hurt. When we returned, Frisky, being the obedient dog that he was, was still in the same spot where Kenny had left him. Kenny and Frisky had a most joyful reunion and then we happily continued on our trip. Frisky never left Kenny's arms again until we were safely at home.

I suppose every mother has a story about a forgotten toy that needed rescue, and mothers don't generally forget those frantic moments. To this day, all anyone in our family has to say is "Roanoke, Alabama" and someone else will smile and say "Frisky," as if that says it all. Now that Kenny is grown, Frisky is again spending his days snoozing on my bed. He can rest easy now; he has done his job, and done it well. He provided Kenny's boyhood years with a feeling of love and contentment, and me with precious memories.

DEBBIE CLEMENT

I cannot imagine a cat in an Obedience ring,
running around in the hot sun
and doing things on command.
Gladys Taber

EARLY MORNING TAKE-OUT

Considering it's a brand-new experience for me, I generally do a fine job of getting my kindergartner ready for the bus by the crack of dawn. But on one unseasonably cold November morning we were running a little behind, mainly because Gabe and his little brother, Blaise, had convinced me that they *needed* pancakes for breakfast. Even so, just before the bus arrived, Gabe was ready to go: shoes on, vitamins down, teeth brushed, coat and backpack on. Blaise and I were still in our pajamas, however. As I was explaining to Gabe that I'd bid him goodbye from the deck, instead of walking him to the end of our driveway, the bus arrived.

I stepped out into the frosty morning in my bare feet to wave as Gabe headed toward the bus. Blaise decided that he needed to be outside, too, but when he opened the door and put his little feet into the bitter cold, my mothering instincts took hold. I fussed at him for coming outside in bare feet and short-sleeved pajamas—just like me. His three-year-old mind concocted a way to please himself and me: he kept his feet inside and leaned forward to push the door wide open.

Our cat, who is declawed in the front and not allowed outside, didn't waste any time in seizing the opportunity to escape. She darted out as though Garfield himself waited on the other side of the door to congratulate her. Gabe saw this and became alarmed, begging me to catch the cat. "I'll take care of it, honey," I said as calmly as I could muster. "You go on and get on the bus." The bus idled roughly at the end of our driveway as Gabe walked toward it with a doubtful, worried look. I decided I'd catch the cat before the bus turned around and came back down our street.

Barefooted and in my pajamas, I darted through some woods in our side yard chasing after our five-pound animal, who led me through a briar patch around to the back of the house. She finally stopped long enough to hiss her disgust with me, and I pounced on her. Just in time, too. The bus was heading back toward our house. "Caught ya!" I yelled triumphantly.

I ran, clutching the cat, to the middle of our driveway and stood there skimpily clad, but undefeated by our feline, in order to show Gabe—and fifty other amused kids and the wide-eyed bus driver. *So what?* I thought. I needed to make sure that Gabe's mind was free to concentrate on the more academic tasks of kindergarten and not a missing cat.

But the cat panicked when he saw the moving vehicle as the busload of curious eyes neared our driveway. She used every bit of her intact back claws to slice up my arms and chest on her way to the ground. My wounds filled me with a fiery determination to not let her escape, so I dove toward the pavement, grabbing her tail. The cat scrambled, but I, with my own tail in the air, held fast with both hands, yanking behind her up the driveway and into the house.

Whew, I did it, I thought, once safely inside with the door closed. Now Gabe won't have to worry. But a cold sweat filled my pores as I recalled the kindergarten's recent journal topic,

"What I Saw on My Way to School Today." Please, God, don't let that be the subject today, I prayed.

When Gabe arrived home that afternoon, he complained that his stomach hurt. I didn't ask if it was because he was teased by other kids due to his mommy's half-clothed, early-morning antics, or if his ache was a result of the pancakes we had for breakfast. From now on though, Pop-Tarts sound like a pretty safe bet.

LEE ANN WOODS

CAUGHT ON FILM

Two dollars and fifty cents. That's the going price for a bunny these days. Our two sons shook the stuffin's out of their piggy banks to come up with just that amount, and the bunny was sold!

This was not just any bunny my sons purchased at an auction they had attended with their father. And after much pondering and discussion, they decided to call this caramel-colored little critter Werther, after the scrumptious candies. A very dignified name indeed.

Werther arrived home in the crook of one son's arm, and the well-established tenants of our acreage, our dog and cat, perked up with great curiosity. The feline soon yawned and became bored with the bunny. The dog, however, circled 'round and 'round poor Werther and barked nonstop until my sons decided the only logical and safe place for Werther to hang out was in a refrigerator box in their bedroom.

It could have been the nuisance of walking around a refrigerator box every time I attempted to put away laundry and make their beds, or perhaps the odor that now characterized their room, that made this mother declare on day three that all bunnies belong outside!

So my eleven-year-old headed down to the barn in the afternoon after school and gathered up all kinds of materials to construct a pen for the bunny. With chicken wire, bricks, fence posts, and firewood logs, he used his imagination to build the most elaborate pen that any bunny could hope, or shall we say "hop," for.

As anyone who has grown up around pets or livestock knows, the animal world is sometimes a cruel and harsh place. This was certainly true in Werther's case. Due to natural causes, our new pet's life was very short.

Even our teenage daughter left the phone alone long enough at the end of the day to help her brothers provide a fitting and well-deserved burial for Werther.

As my husband and I sat at the kitchen table, we watched the funeral procession march across the yard and head down toward the timber. Three children, one bunny gently laid in a shovel, and one wooden cross constructed by small hands. With the sun beginning to set on this gentle spring day, we watched them disappear as they set off to conduct their own service. We uttered not a word, just anxiously watched for them to reappear. And soon they did—this time sister carrying the empty shovel and little brother riding on his big brother's back.

Now, why would my partner in child rearing and I be unable to speak or look across the table at each other without becoming blubbering idiots? This was only a $2.50 bunny, for goodness sake! But it was so much more. It was one of those Kodak moments that pulled at our heartstrings. A snapshot engraved in our minds. We sat and witnessed the fruits of our labor—our children loving the bunny, loving one another, and seeking each other out with open arms during a tough time in their young lives.

CHRISTI KROMMINGA

THE DIVORCE DOG

*C*asey was taken to an animal shelter at age ten by owners who were getting divorced. She wasn't on any list of disputed property or part of the settlement. She was just on the list of things to get rid of before the house was sold.

I got the call from the shelter the same afternoon.

"We weren't going to call you because of her age," said the girl, "but we thought we'd give it a try."

"I'll come out this afternoon," I told her.

Why didn't I tell her to put the old dog to sleep? As a representative of the local Collie Rescue effort, I had picked up many dogs from various shelters, but never a ten-year-old. Why was I putting myself through making eye contact with the old dog, touching her, only to tell them she wouldn't be adopted and that I couldn't take her? I had a picture in my head of what I expected to see when I got there: an arthritic, gray-in-the-face, beaten-down, sick, old dog. I wasn't even close.

The girl took me to the back room where injured animals were kept. Casey was standing in her kennel run as if waiting for someone to open the door. I took her out on a leash and began my evaluation while the girl watched and we talked. Casey understood basic commands and was easily handled. I asked her to lie down and she did, with ease. But now the big test: could she get up from the floor? I called her name from a few feet away. We laughed when Casey shot up from the floor and ran past me, pulling on the leash to leave.

Casey was in the back of my car a few minutes later. I couldn't leave her when she had such a strong will to go, but I couldn't help wondering what the rest of the rescue group would say when I told them I had picked up a ten-year-old dog.

Casey got a bath, and her dark black coat was dematted and brushed till it flowed around her body. I kept her isolated from my own collies in case she carried something contagious from the shelter.

"She's been spayed for quite some time," the veterinarian said later that week, "and she's blind in one eye." How was Collie Rescue ever going to find a home for an old, half-blind dog?

Surprisingly, the rescue group agreed to keep Casey, and I let her go into foster care with another board member. After three months, the board member began divorce proceedings. I expected that Casey would have to move into a second foster home when, out of the blue, a nice young couple adopted her.

Casey moved into her new home, and we all did high fives and moved on to picking up more collies to place. A year went by before we got the news. The young couple was getting divorced, and Casey was coming back to us at age eleven. After all this, we couldn't help but call her the "Divorce Dog."

What was wrong with Casey that everyone who owned her got divorced? Absolutely nothing. She was a pretty collie with the look of good breeding. She slept a good portion of the day but could walk a good distance and be playful if you wanted her to. She fit in well with other dogs and got along with cats. She had no bad habits or vices, but this divorce thing that followed her around seemed kind of, well, weird.

Our policy to evaluate each dog on its own merit, regardless of age, wasn't looking like a workable policy. No one came to Rescue asking for an old dog on its last leg; they wanted a Lassie who would live till the children went off to college. If we couldn't get old dogs new homes, they could become our own old dogs by default, and we couldn't keep doing that either.

Our next newsletter featured Casey, and lo and behold, a couple that owned two collies made an inquiry about her. We decided not to mention the divorce thing. She showed all her best qualities to the new couple and they liked her. If she got along with their two young collies, they would give a home to this old girl.

So Casey went off to her third home. We wouldn't have been surprised if we heard of her passing that year, or the next. But magically, Casey's home-breaking days were over. The docile old girl began to weave her way into many hearts.

Instead of getting a call about her passing, we heard about her daily walks on the grounds of the local university, where she impressed people with her gentle collie ways. Casey became an ambassador for the breed.

At fourteen, Casey still walked every day, but she decided when the walk was over by turning around and heading home. Then came the call that she had had several mini-strokes. When her owners had to return to work the next day, I went and sat with Casey. I thought the end was near, and I didn't want her to be alone. But she recovered.

After that, I became her daytime caregiver and went to her home every weekday at noon to let her outside. Many times I had to wake her from a deep sleep and massage her hindquarters to warm up the muscles. She wobbled, then walked sedately outside to the yard. I left her curled up on the sofa to begin her afternoon nap.

A neighbor said God had forgotten Casey, but I felt God was blessing her owners for their compassion. Even though she became deaf, her owners whispered in her ear as they hugged her, "It's okay to die, Casey." She ignored their permission and lived on for another year.

At seventeen, Casey was a collie with presence. Supremely in command, as though her longevity gave her the right, she ruled her house of collies, yet played with them lovingly. She made everyone laugh. And she never missed a meal, a treat, a walk, or an opportunity to bark in the window.

It was a beautiful Sunday in May, when the world outside was bursting into bloom with new life, that God finally remembered Casey and called her home. She went peacefully.

That was three years ago. I'm raising a new collie puppy of my own these days. He's full of spice. I get this feeling of gladness in my heart when I watch his puppy antics. It's the same feeling I got every time I saw Casey. If he doesn't swallow any more really bad things this year, there is a good chance his vinegar and spice will turn into the fine wine that is an old dog.

LINDA L. S. KNOUSE

A DIFFERENT KIND
OF MOTHER

Mothers come in as many varieties as snack chips. There are birth mothers, stepmothers, adopted mothers, working mothers, stay-at-home moms, surrogate mothers, single mothers, part-time mothers, and foster mothers. A friend of mine is "Mama" to her niece and nephew. And I read a recent news article about grandmothers who are raising their children's children.

I spent the morning just after New Year's rummaging through dictionaries, encyclopedias, and other reference books in hopes of validating my place in this list, my place among the mothers.

Although no ringlet-headed toddler scatters fingerprints on my walls, my five-year-old leaves her toys in the middle of the living room and crawls into bed with me at the first boom of a thunderstorm.

Kia is a service dog, which means she is specially trained to help someone with a disability. Unlike a pet dog, she goes everywhere with me, so I am responsible for her behavior in public. I have always felt like a mother, specifically her mother, so I decided to prove that I am.

According to my Merriam-Webster dictionary, a scarred and yellowed high school graduation gift, a mother is a female parent or a woman who has given birth. I glanced down at Kia lying under the table. Nope, not me.

I checked the *World Scope Encyclopedia*—no mother there. The *New York Public Library Desk Reference* offered nothing either, so I heaved the *Reader's Digest Encyclopedic Dictionary* open with a thud.

My hopes of finding validation were waning as I flipped the pages—"miff," "more," "move"—go back—"mother: noun," more of the same, then I read, "A female who has adopted a child or otherwise established a relationship with another person." Kia stretched and did a full-body shake, rattling the brass buckles on her harness.

"It's not perfect, but I did sign papers," I reminded myself. "That counts as an adoption, doesn't it?" She plopped down with an unconvinced sigh, so I kept reading:

"5) a woman having some of the responsibilities of a mother."

As a service dog, Kia has to be worked daily to keep her skills sharp. I also take her to obedience school and teach her new skills. I discipline her when needed and monitor her health, seeing that she gets her pills and plenty of exercise. I make sure she has playtime and, of course, that she goes to the bathroom before we go someplace. What could be more motherly than that?

"6) qualities attributed to a mother, such as the capacity to love selflessly."

I peeked down at Kia, her eyelids drooping slowly as she fought sleep. When she caught me watching, the tip of her tail flicked on the carpet. Yeah, this one fit.

I love her for the dozen things she does for me daily and for her willingness to learn more. I love her because when she's playing, she always wants me to watch. She wants me with her.

She loves me because I feed her, groom her, and praise her when she does something good. She depends on me; I depend on her. The love is unquestionable.

"3) verb, to watch over, nourish, and protect."

I literally watch Kia all the time. I like to watch her run in the yard and then watch her sleeping with her nose twitching and paws fluttering as she chases a squirrel through her dreams.

I watched her check out a crab on a boat tour of St. Simons

Sound one summer, and I watched her crawl under my wheel-chair's footstools to avoid the strobe light at a B-52s concert a couple of years ago.

If Kia sleeps too long, I watch to see if she's still breathing. Once I had a dream that she got hurt. Panicked, I woke her to be sure she was okay.

We were chased one day by a loose and angry dog. Knowing I couldn't run the dog off myself and that Kia, attached to my wheelchair, wouldn't have a chance in a fight, I simply took off as fast as my chair could go.

Not wanting to frighten her, I kept my voice calm, repeating "It's okay. You're okay. Let's go . . ." until the other dog turned back. Kia must have believed me, because when we got home she plopped down on her bed for a nap as always. It took me the rest of the day to stop shaking.

I sat back from my note-taking and smiled. The morning was nearly gone, but I had found my validation. I complied, with a little creative license, to the definitions in that book. *I am a mother and I can prove it,* I thought triumphantly.

Just then my black, furry bundle of joy knocked my elbow, bouncing my hand onto her head for a rub.

"What, Baby-Dawg?" I asked as my pen dropped to the floor. She whirled to grab it, dropping it in my lap without even a toothmark in the barrel.

"Good girl, thank you." I rubbed under her chin.

Wag, wag, wag went her whole behind, then she reared back to put her feet on my knees, slurping a kiss up my chin as she came. "Who needs proof, Mom?"

Not me. Not anymore.

AMY MUNNELL

RUNNING FREE

I stood and watched, tears streaming down my face. The old man sauntered down the street, my beloved German shepherd, Cheyenne, trotting by his side.

"Did she have to go so willingly?" I sobbed.

"It's better for her," my husband soothed.

"But she doesn't know she isn't coming back," I wailed.

"Don't be too sure." My husband drew me into his arms. "She's a smart dog."

I thought about the day we brought her home. She was fat and goofy-looking, almost black, while one ear stood straight up and the other drooped lazily. Within the hour, she wet on the kitchen floor. I rubbed her nose in it and set her none too gently outside. It never happened again in four years, except once after her surgery to get spayed.

As Cheyenne grew, she slimmed down. Her color changed. Her chest was almond, turning to shades of brown on the sides, with a black saddle. She was a beauty with her own distinct personality.

Cheyenne loved to go for walks. As soon as the leash tinkled, she'd be anxious to leave. Each time we went to the city park, she'd run back and forth, end to end across the small grassy area as if looking for even more freedom to romp in.

Cheyenne seemed to stay forever puppylike. Even as she aged, she would run, tail wagging, to welcome visitors. She seldom barked, and growled only once. I was awed by her gentle ways. I had grown up on a farm and had worked with many dogs. Never had I met one like Cheyenne. Many times I marveled at her depth of understanding.

One night when my husband was at work, a man he worked with dropped by. When I opened the door, Cheyenne trotted through the living room and stood by my side. I noticed at the time that her stance was somewhat stiff. Her ears were up, tail down. I'd never seen her take that particular position before.

Wary of her intentions, I slipped my fingers under her collar. Then I heard it, the rumble deep in her throat. I tightened my hold on her and spoke to her. Though she stopped growling, she put her head down and crouched.

Calmly I told the man that my husband was working overtime. He looked at me strangely. "I'll just come in and wait," he said.

As he tried to push his way past me, Cheyenne leapt forward, pulling me after her. Her vicious snarls made my blood run cold. I braced my body and pulled her back.

"I think you should go," I said, realizing the man was intoxicated.

After he left, I patted Cheyenne's head and hugged her neck. I'd only seen this man once before, but his actions made me wonder what his intentions had been. If Cheyenne hadn't wanted him in the house, I now trusted she had good cause.

When my husband came home, and I told him about our visitor, he said the man knew all along that he was working. Months later, we found out this coworker was wanted by the police in another part of the country.

Cheyenne and I spent many happy hours together. We played ball, went to the park, and in the evenings she'd curl up at my feet.

The following summer I was in an auto accident, and we were forced to move. Cheyenne couldn't go because we were moving to an apartment.

I cried for over a week after Cheyenne left with the old man.

She'd been my friend, companion, and protector. I felt as if someone had ripped my heart out.

A few months later, I was busy upstairs in our new place. Someone knocked loudly on the door. When I opened it, a brown streak jumped up at me. Large paws hit my chest. A tongue lapped my face. I was ecstatic. It was Cheyenne and her master.

"How'd you know where we lived?" I asked in wonder.

"Cheyenne knew. We were walking by, and she recognized the car. Raised such a fuss, I had to see if it was really yours."

"I'm glad you did," I replied, smiling. And I meant every word.

That day we arranged for Cheyenne to come for visits every other Saturday. The old man would chat with my husband while Cheyenne and I went for a walk or played ball in the yard. The bond that had been broken was soon firmly in place once again.

Though the old man died two years later, I was able to keep track of Cheyenne. She now lives in the country with a couple and their four children.

She no longer comes to visit, but twice a year I phone to see how she is doing. In the winter she pulls the children in a sled, and in the summer she patrols the property and bounds through the fields.

Even after seven years, I think of her often. When I do, a tear rolls down my cheek. I swipe it away and chastise myself for being so selfish. After all, she no longer has to spend hours on a chain or be controlled by a leash.

Sometimes I close my eyes, and I can see her running after a rabbit, flying across acres of farmland. Then I smile, knowing I did the right thing by letting her go. She's free at last.

MARY M. ALWARD

IV
THE ANSWERS ARE WITHIN

Letting go is like releasing a tight spring at the core of yourself,

one you've spent your whole life winding and maintaining.

When you let go, you grow still and quiet. You learn to sit

among the cornstalks and wait with God.

SUE MONK KIDD

A GIRL NAMED TOMM

When my first daughter was born in Israel twenty-four years ago, her father and I were riding the last ebb of the '60s as it manifested itself in a country where the young—so unlike our counterparts in the United States—did not need to rebel against their elders. After all, we were the generation that five years earlier had won the Six-Day War.

Our only act of defiance against our families came in the choice of a name for our child. We named our daughter Tomm.

In Hebrew, the word means purity of the heart, innocence, like the trusting smile of a baby. But the noun was not used to name a girl. The innocence, we knew, would not hold well for the grandmother she one day would become. And being in the throes of preparations to move to the United States, the complications of carrying this name were not lost on us. But we liked the ring of the word and the values it represented.

She was not yet two years old at the time we arrived here. With a short, closely trimmed, French-style haircut; a quick smile; and an outgoing demeanor, she often encountered the inquiries of well-meaning strangers.

"What a nice little boy you are," someone would say to her in the supermarket.

At ages three and four she was used to it. "I'm not a boy, I'm a girl," she would correct patiently.

"Of course! What a cute girl. What's your name?"

"Tomm."

The stranger would then send an awkward glance in my direction, perhaps sympathizing with me for having a child suffering a gender-identity crisis at such a young age.

Since middle names were uncommon in Israel, I came up with an idea. "Tommie, why don't you pick up a middle name and that's the name we'll use?"

I expected her to choose "Lisa" or "Jennifer." Instead, at her first week in kindergarten, she announced, "The teacher says I have a wonderful middle name."

"What is it?"

"Happy. My name now is Happy Tomm."

I swallowed hard. Not wanting to stifle either her budding creativity or her profuse optimism, I faintly offered, "No one's named Happy."

"I am."

Right. I continued to call her Tomm and its many derivations—sometimes stretching it, Eastern European style, to Tommchkiniu—hoping that in time she would exercise her option for a new name in a more conventional way.

When she was in second grade, I noticed that she added "L" as a middle initial.

"What does the *L* stand for?" I asked casually, hoping she had finally chosen "Lisa."

"Love."

"Uh?"

"My name is Tomm Love."

Facing such assurance of a girl grooving her own life's path, I let it slide.

It took me a while to figure out that with her limited knowledge of Hebrew, she translated the "innocence of heart," *Tomm-Lev,* to "love." She could not have picked a better name to suit her even-tempered nature.

A couple of years later, with a move to a new school, I seized the opportunity to undo the lifelong damage I might have inflicted upon my child. "Would you like to pick a new name?" I asked.

"I like Love," replied my preadolescent daughter, and I feared the coming teenage years, which would, on top of real problems, bring invented angst. But she rolled the words off her tongue, tasting them. "Tomm Love."

With no practical alternatives, I continued to call her Tomm, by now a too-strong syllable that, to my ear, sounded dissonant with the softer notion of love.

The benefits of having an unusual name became evident when, at sixteen, she met a young man at the local record store and they spent time talking.

"He didn't ask for my phone number," she lamented later.

"With your name, he'll find you if he wants to."

If he had half a brain, he would want to, of course. Happy Tomm Love had developed into a striking beauty with an engaging—and, yes, lovable—personality. Sure enough, the young man inquired at the high school, and called her the next day.

A few years ago, I overheard a conversation between Tomm and her younger sister, Eden, who had not endured years of raised eyebrows. Both agreed that they were proud of their unusual first names and would never subject their children to the indignity of sharing their names with multitudes of others.

"Can you imagine having a name that twenty other girls have?" Eden asked.

"It would take away a part of who you are," Tomm replied.

Upon graduating from college, Tomm began her job search.

"Maybe you should have added a 'Miss' in front of your name on the résumé," I remarked the morning I drove her to the train for her first interview. For all I knew, they did not expect this sweet-demeanor female to walk in the door.

"What's the difference?" Tomm replied. She gave me a bright smile and a peck on the cheek and climbed out of the car, ready to face life.

She did not hear my silent "Go get them." She would get them, I knew. To this born winner, her name had been an unintentional gift, a pole to use in vaulting over any of life's hurdles.

TALIA CARNER

I didn't leave you for another man.
I left you for another woman—
the one I couldn't be while I was with you.
<small>Ellen Hansen</small>

COMING HOME

The coyotes were singing down by the canal on the night that I tried to come home. As I crept up the driveway lining the meadow, the cinders beneath my feet crunched loudly, broadcasting my guilt. Moonlight bathed the juniper trees in its silvery sheen; they lined up to witness my return. The wind carried their scent to me and I inhaled deeply the exotic aroma of the high desert, then I tiptoed up the porch steps to the house that we once shared.

I found myself quivering on the doorstep.

My fist raised, ready to knock, I paused. I pressed my body against the rough siding and willed the molecules to dissolve—to allow me to pass through the wood, back into the life we shared. "Forgive me," I would say when you opened, "and I'll forgive you."

I heard your familiar step on the floor, coming closer to where I crouched in the light of the moon, crying. Afraid of the sound of your voice, the anger in your eyes, I backed away. I ran wildly down the driveway to my car. I drove away. Fast.

The road that stretched out ahead of me was unfamiliar, but

exciting. As the yellow lines zipped past and the years fell away, I began to find bits of myself lying alongside the road. I stopped and gathered them up. My eyes remained on the path ahead, but I sometimes wondered what might have been.

Years later, while on a long drive, I returned—in my imagination—to the house we once shared.

I walk quietly past the pasture where we might have kept a horse. The sun peeks over the rooftop of the house where we might have raised a family, and bathes the yard in yellow light. I can almost see the Easter egg hunts we might have had there in the spring, and the snowmen we might have built in the winter.

Quivering on the doorstep, I knock. And this time, you answer. Your forehead is creased. I used to massage those worry lines away, years ago. But not today. Resisting the urge to smooth your bushy eyebrows, I look into your soft brown eyes. I see you in there, buried beneath the scars of your experience, but you don't see me. You look right through me, into the mirror at the back of my eyes. You judge me according to your own motivations and thoughts. You don't like what you see. There is no love in your eyes—not for me.

Shoulders back, voice strong: Forgive me, I say. And know that I forgive you. I'm leaving now. You hold the memory of my innocence, but you don't hold me. I loved you, but we needed more than hope and fruitless effort. Goodbye, my first love. Goodbye. Turning with my head held high in the bright morning sun, I step lightly back to my car. I drive slowly away.

Back in my own driveway, I jump out of the car and run across the lawn to the front door. Just before I fling it open, I pause and press my ear against it. Inside, I hear the voices of my children, playing. Softly, I open the door and am greeted by the scent of morning coffee and crispy wheat toast. There is one moment of complete silence, then the sounds of running feet, voices calling, "Mommy's home!"

Stooping down, first on one knee and then both, I gather my children into my arms. Looking up, I see my husband's eyes, smiling into mine. Sometimes you have to say goodbye before you can come home.

LUCI N. FULLER

A PLACE TO BE

My *childhood friend and I went to a certain* place almost every day after school when we were in the third grade. The setting was beautiful, surrounded by huge box elder trees, aspens, and Scotch pines. The Logan River ran through the abandoned park and old farm equipment lay scattered like someone's forgotten toys. We had to walk under five giant cement arches each time we went to our place in order to ceremoniously "enter the grounds." Together we shared the adventures that only children can dream up and understand.

We named our place Dominicia because we thought it sounded mysterious, regal, and even powerful. Each day our quest was to find something, anything, that was different from our normal routine. I can't begin to count how many hillsides we dug into looking for lost colonies or dinosaur bones, or the piles of rocks we collected because we knew that there must be gold in the middle of one of the rocks, or, at the very least, one had to hold some kind of magic power. Our days were sweet with anticipation for the next big discovery, time being the enemy of sorts because dusk always came too soon.

I remember hearing the word *cancer* for the first time. They kept saying that my dad had cancer. For a young girl, that word was dark and terrifying. Not wanting to scare me, no one would talk to me any further about it. But really, not knowing scared me more than anything else.

During that time, I found myself escaping to Dominicia more and more. My friend seemed to understand my need for solitude, so I went alone. In Dominicia, I felt calm as I listened to the wind twist through tree branches and the river fall over the rocks in its path. I could be alone to work through the maze of fears and worries that constantly swirled in my brain without having to look at people shake their heads and offer half smiles of sympathy. In Dominicia, I had a place to be. A place to be scared, brave, heroic, or simply a nine-year-old girl.

For three years I sought refuge from my dad's reality in the imaginary walls of Dominicia. I learned more about his condition, and he promised me that he would win the horrible battle he was fighting. I had never known my dad to go back on a promise, but sometimes that gave little comfort because everything felt completely overwhelming to me. I just knew that dad was very sick, and I desperately wanted him to get better.

The first cement arch was built close to one of the many hillsides that surrounded Dominicia. Many times I would slide down the face of the hill and climb to the top of the first arch, as close to Heaven as I could get, and I would pray that Dad would beat the cancer that was hurting him. I prayed into the heavens, expressing my wishes the only way I knew how, and hoped that I would be heard above the rest of the people in the world.

I remember the first time I heard the word *remission*. Three years later, they were saying my dad was in remission. Then other phrases came along like "getting better," "doing well," and finally "cured." People's smiles were real, and I knew that Dad had kept his promise.

I continued to go to Dominicia, but not to escape anymore. I began to go with my friend again, and we, in a way, were able to pick up where we left off. Things had changed a bit, but so had I. And on the occasions I did go alone, I would climb to the top of the arch. When I reached the top, I'd sit and look at the world below me as thin breezes touched my face. In the silence, I would breathe a prayer of gratitude and then stand up on the arch to somehow show that I wasn't afraid anymore.

It's been well over two decades since I walked beneath the arches into Dominicia, and my dad has continued to keep his promise. Sometimes I think that I ought to go back and see if the place looks the same. Maybe I could find some of the treasures my friend and I buried at the bases of the huge trees. Maybe I could take my son, and we could dig for those elusive dinosaur bones. Or maybe, if I felt brave enough, I could let go of the gravity of adulthood and climb to the top of that first cement arch where so many years before I offered up my childhood fears to the skies.

JaNell Davis Mathews

MIRROR IMAGE

*T*he day I got fitness as a religion was the day I thought all my problems were solved. The fat girl in the mirror wasn't running my life with her side pains and shortness of breath anymore. I was twenty-three, nursing a three-month-old, and still stretching out the front panel of my maternity pants.

I showed up for my first aerobics class in homemade elastic-waist shorts and my husband's baggy V-neck T-shirt. All the women in their tights and leotards showing off trim legs and bellies stood in tight knots, visiting. I staked out an empty spot as close to the back wall as possible and bent over to touch my toes. I couldn't. Forty minutes of jump, kick, and twirl left my legs and arms leaden and my clothes sweated clean through. Some of the leotard ladies barely broke a sweat.

At home I took a tape measure to my lumpy hips and thighs, to the first real breasts I'd ever had, but they were lost in proportion to the rest of me. I wrote down the numbers and stuffed them into my bathroom drawer next to the full-length mirror. I cut all fat from my diet, began making my own yogurt, and watched my breast milk go from full cream to skim.

By my daughter's six-month birthday, my body began to take shape. Maternity pants and muumuus went to Goodwill. I bought jeans with a button fly, started doing biceps curls with soup cans while I read up on low-fat foods, and exercised during my daughter's naps.

On my daughter's first birthday, I skipped the cake and ice

cream and took out the tape measure. I'd lost a little over two inches off my hips, and had dropped another jeans size. In the mirror I flexed a biceps, a calf, and saw the power of what I'd done—and also the cellulite on my rear and the Pillsbury stomach that refused to flatten. *Just lose a few more pounds,* I thought, *then I can slow down.* One afternoon a few months later, my mother-in-law asked, "Are you eating enough?" I laughed and swung my daughter around the way she loved. "I'm serious," my mother-in-law said, "your face is getting too thin." My husband had mentioned this once, but I told him, "You're just not used to it, that's all."

The next day I bought myself a pair of size-six lavender jeans to celebrate, but the celebration didn't last long. I was pregnant again and panicked at the thought of starting all over with my body once the baby arrived. Early in the pregnancy aerobics made me nauseous, so I took up swimming laps for forty minutes daily.

My husband said, "Ease up."

My mother-in-law said, "Think of the baby."

"What could be better for a baby than a healthy mother?" I replied.

My doctor said, "Eat red meat; don't swim more than three times a week. You don't need any more than that to keep you fit." What did he know? He was the one who told me to eat anything I wanted during my first pregnancy, that the weight would melt right off with breast-feeding. I cut back the swimming to four days a week to keep everybody happy.

When my son arrived, he was six and a half pounds and healthy. My doctor released me to do aerobics again when my son was three months old, but after a few months, my initial enthusiasm just wasn't there. Although I was healthy and my clothes fit, I still felt fat. No matter how complimentary the tape measure was, the mirror spoke to the contrary. My rear still jiggled, my stomach still wouldn't go concave when I sucked it in, the proportions were all off. If I could just lose another few pounds I'd be fine.

When I felt tired or caught myself slacking off, I worked harder. In addition to aerobics five days a week, I ran on weekends. My husband didn't say a word, neither did my mother-in-law, but my doctor recommended solids and supplemental formula for my son at six months because he wasn't gaining enough weight on breast milk alone. I made the switch and worked harder. By my son's first birthday, the mirror reflected a child's torso. My collarbone, ribs, and shoulder blades were all contours and lines, taut skin in between. I stopped wearing a bra because I didn't need one. I wore bulky, long sweaters to hide my thinness from family and friends. I knew I was getting too thin, but what I knew how to do was lose weight, not how to stop.

At close to a hundred pounds, circumstance intervened. I broke a knee snow skiing. My brother drove me off the mountain and delivered me to an empty house because my husband and kids were visiting friends out of state. I was trapped with myself for the weekend. I holed up in the living room, took the Vicadan the doctor on the mountain had given me, and talked myself into believing nothing was wrong that a couple of weeks off wouldn't fix.

The following week a series of doctors' exams and MRIs revealed extensive damage and the need for reconstructive knee surgery. I couldn't believe it. I'd been so strong and now I needed help with the most basic things. A glass of water couldn't be carried back from the kitchen on crutches; the stairs to my bedroom became a hazard even though I now took them one, instead of two, at a time. I beat my metal crutches on the floor until one bent. I railed at friends calling to offer sympathy and help. I snapped at my husband when he tried to anticipate my needs, and finally, the day before I went in for surgery, in spite of the presence of family and friends, I found myself completely alone.

In the weeks and months that followed, my ankle-to-hip knee brace gave me plenty of time to think. I could think of nothing the same way because physically I was a different person. I wasn't the fat girl, but I also wasn't the strong woman either. For a few months, I was nothing, just this very small woman who camped on the couch waiting for something to fill the void. One day, as I sat watching spring rain slide down the windows, I realized nothing would come to me. I'd have to do something. I'd have to ask. Healing, I prayed, just give me healing.

Because I was ignorant of the power of sincere prayer, I didn't realize the course my life would take once I uttered that simple request. Help had been waiting in the wings all along, I just hadn't seen it. A conversation with my husband and a few phone calls started me in counseling and physical therapy. As my knee healed, my mind made the discovery that I am not my body and that health is how I feel about myself no matter what the mirror reflects.

My most valuable exercise these days is gratitude.

BURKY ACHILLES

THE MUSTARD SEED

My husband and I had enjoyed raising our family in San Fernando Valley, California. Yet, as retirement neared, we felt we needed to live in a quieter, cooler area. We began house-hunting farther north along the coast.

During the years that I had been thinking about our retirement home, a set of mental "specs" had evolved. We needed a two-story house (for cardiovascular exercise), a den/bedroom downstairs (to use as an office), two *large* bedrooms upstairs (each with its own bath), and a kitchen area that gave me something interesting to look at. There should be no yard work for us to do (after all, we had mowed a yard for years). Oh, yes, a crystal chandelier in the dining room, a fireplace, and a water view would be nice!

As I began praying for our dream home, the Bible I had in my hands fell open to Matthew 17:20: ". . . if you have faith as a grain of mustard seed, you will say to this mountain, 'move hence to yonder place,' and it will move; and nothing will be impossible to you." I thought, *Yes, Lord, that's right. All I need to do is to have faith.* On impulse, I went out and bought a pair of pillowcases for our future bedroom, some pot holders for the kitchen, and a crystal lamp finial for the living room.

I shouldn't have been surprised when one day our real estate agent led us to a house on a marina that exceeded my expectations. It had main channel water views from the kitchen, living room, and master bedroom. Instead of a backyard, there was a large redwood deck! All the rooms were exactly as I had prayed for! The kitchen counters were thirty-seven inches high—a loving Heavenly Father had even provided a comfortable working height for a tall woman.

We went happily into escrow. Then a period of testing began. We had planned to sell a piece of property and use that as a part of the down payment, but it stubbornly refused to sell. We tried everything. One day, in desperation, we talked to the vice president of a small local valley bank near us. As we explained our problem, the man began to smile. He had relatives in the town our new house was in, and he went jogging on weekends over the bridge near our dream home. He knew *exactly* where it was and what it was worth. He told us to pick up our "swing loan" check the next day on our signatures only. We floated home.

We have been happily retired for some years now. I often think of that blessed day when the Realtor took us to our dream house. The significance of Matthew 17:20 became apparent even before I stepped over the threshold. There, beside the front door, a previous owner had written in the cement: THE MUSTARD SEED.

PATRICIA ANAND

A GIFT OF GRACE

It's been several years since I held my newborn baby while she died. Our daughter Grace was born very prematurely. In fact, she was born just seventeen gestational days before the miracles of modern medicine can save preterm infants. She was just too small to survive.

Still hemorrhaging from delivery, I simply rocked our baby to her death thirty-two minutes later. There was nothing else to do.

As you can imagine, my grief was immense. It was unspeakable. But gradually, I realized that I wanted Grace to have a healthy family. And healthy meant healing. I found it particularly difficult, though, to reconcile my faith with this tragedy. After all, what kind of God kills little babies?

My anguish was made worse just four months later when I heard a news account of another premature baby born in Miami at about the same gestational age and birth weight as Grace. Unlike our medical specialists, this baby's doctors did try heroic measures. Now this little girl was going home with her mother that very same day!

I was fed up. With the world. With God. With everything I had believed in. I guess my faith had been somewhat childlike in that I really thought that as long as you did good deeds—were a good person—you would be protected from harm. But the injustice of my situation when compared to this other mother's was just too much. My entire belief system crashed.

That night I told my friends what had happened. I was furious at God for "killing" my baby. I let them know I was giving God twenty-four hours to explain this inequity or be *out* forever. Finally, I demanded that God's explanation be *big!* "After all," I went on, "I'm grieving and not likely to notice some little esoteric message."

Just three hours later, I was at home alone with my dead baby's ashes when the phone rang. It was a stranger calling me in Virginia from Colorado. He needed my help.

Apparently, one of his employees had a girlfriend who was new to my area. She was ill and needed to see a doctor. When she could not reach her boyfriend, she called his boss in Colorado and gave him my name. It seems she and I had met recently, and I had given her my card. I was the only person she "knew" locally.

Sick with my own misery and grief, I offered to drive this stranger to a nearby hospital—the very one where our daughter had been born.

Once there, we discovered that the hospital was so busy there was no room to put us. The only room available was the emergency labor and delivery room!

Later they did move us—to the emergency pediatric ward. Imagine my anguish at being surrounded by all of those beautiful, living babies just down the hallway from the morgue where I had left mine.

At one point, I looked out of our room. I was surprised to see my coworker, Candy, in the room directly across from ours. Her own baby was sick and needed emergency care. As I looked across at Candy she was holding down her terrified, screaming baby while the doctor tried to insert an intravenous line.

Just then, Candy looked up and noticed me across the way. Our eyes connected with the unspoken knowing of a mother whose child is suffering and yet is powerless to help.

As I looked at Candy, I was filled with sudden understanding. And in that moment, I knew peace.

You see, while Candy's baby could scream in pain, mine would have suffered hers in silent agony—Grace had not yet developed the ability to make noise.

While Candy's baby was surrounded and comforted by people who loved her, my baby, if she could have survived at all, would have endured months of silent agony in an isolated incubator. It would have been the only chance she had.

With a flash of knowing, I saw that I had performed the most selfless act of my life. I had loved my baby enough to let her die. Two weeks later I was pregnant again.

One of the things I grieved after Grace's death was that, because she lived for such a short time, she would never be known, that her life was meaningless. I am grateful that a very wise friend said to me, "Jennifer, don't you know? Grace's eternity is that *you* are changed forever. And from this moment forward, everything you do and every life you touch will be different because your life has been touched by Grace. Grace lives on, Jennifer, through you."

Today, I see the wisdom of his words. Although Grace lived for such a short time—indeed, most of us spend longer getting dressed each morning than Grace's entire lifetime—she leaves a powerful legacy of faith, hope, and triumph.

Imagine what we, who are so richly blessed with freedom and fellowship, with love and prosperity, and most of all with time . . . imagine what we could accomplish!

Oh, and by the way—the sick woman I helped that night? I never did see or hear from her again.

It wasn't about her anyway. It was about Grace.

JENNIFER BOYKIN

WHAT DO YOU DO?

I was sitting in the Seattle office of a national auto insurance company, answering routine questions to complete a new policy application, when the process turned into a major identity crisis.

"Employment?" the agent droned, concentrating on his computer screen.

"I just moved here from New York," I said brightly. "I don't have a job yet, so just put unemployed."

"But what's your field?" he asked, turning to look at me.

"Well, I'm not sure what I'm going to do. I'm still looking for a job."

He and his computer stared at me blankly. My smile faded. Apparently, "unemployed" and "undecided" were not two of my options. He repeated his question, certain that I could give a better answer. "But what do you *do*?"

I shifted in my seat, suddenly uncomfortable. "Uh, well . . . um . . ." I had to pick something, but what? I didn't have a "career"; I'd held a variety of jobs. I was starting to feel inadequate, unsuccessful. Why didn't I have the right answer? I sat in fretful silence until my husband came to my rescue.

"She's a writer," he said confidently.

Pacified, the agent typed "writer" into my profile. My husband's reply made the agent happy, and to my relief, it made me happy too. I *was* a writer—I just wasn't making money from writing, so I wasn't sure it counted. Evidently it counted enough to insure my car for liability, comprehensive, and collision.

This wasn't the first time I'd been challenged with the conversation starter "What do you do?" or its evil cousin "What are you?" If I was unemployed, I felt sheepish admitting it. I didn't have a professional title that stands up to unemployment like "doctor" or "attorney." If I was employed, it usually wasn't much to write home about. I wished that just once, someone would open a conversation with something original, like "You seem so organized. Do you do closets?"

Unfortunately, it doesn't work that way. "What do you do?" is still the question of choice, supposedly a quick and easy way to assess who we are. But that day in the insurance office, I learned a new way to answer that age-old question. My simple discovery—that I could explain who I was with my heart's passion, not my job title—was freeing, though a little scary. I decided to start answering the world's questions with what I felt in my heart.

I tried out my new self-definition slowly and tentatively. I signed a membership contract at a new gym, and, predictably, the sales rep asked about my career.

"I just moved here, so I'm still job-hunting," I said, "but I'm a writer."

My response came out more like a question than a statement, but she smiled, wrote down my answer, and asked me more about my favorite topic. Happily, I talked to her about writing. I imagined all the other people like me who must be out there somewhere—secretaries who were really dancers, teachers who lived to play in jazz bands, lawyers in love with community theater. I had been shy before, but now I would start speaking up for us all.

I told my hairdresser I was writing a book. I told my best friends that I had submitted an article to a magazine in hopes of publication. I talked to my husband about the characters in my novel. Opening up about what I loved and defining myself from my heart rather than my job title felt risky—what would people think?—but it became easier and more fun with practice. Newly employed, I now had a job title, but I was determined to not use it as a crutch. *Why do people rely so heavily on careers to make conversation?* I wondered. Jobs are a part of life, not a sole defining characteristic of identity. I vowed to ask my events coordinator friend about her soccer games and my art director friend about her singing performances.

Recently I received a call from a friend who is a doctoral student at Northwestern University, completing her Ph.D. in bacteriology. We talked about many things, and then the conversation turned to a mutual friend who had just earned yet another promotion at a major New York City magazine.

"Did you hear about her job?" she asked.

"Pretty incredible, huh? She's senior art director!"

"Yeah, she's worked her way up to senior art director, and I'm still in school! By the time I get out, I'll be so desperate for a job that some corporation is going to love me. I'll say, 'Twenty thousand dollars a year and a sixty-hour workweek? Sign me up!' "

Now, this is a pretty and well-liked woman earning her Ph.D. who is on the brink of venturing into the world as a research scientist to help find cures for diseases. If *she* worries about falling short of society's expectations of success, anyone could. And I thought I was the only one of my friends who had been worried about being successful enough.

It was comforting to know that all people have doubts about their lives, but even more comforting was the realization that success doesn't have to come from the "right" job or salary. When I decided to define myself by my positive qualities and my passions, I didn't have to wait for the world to grant me the right position or title. I was already successful! I just wish I had known that when applying for car insurance.

ALAINA SMITH

V
SOME KIND OF
WONDERFUL

How shall we find love?

It is ours in that instant when we give it away.

Joan Walsh Anglund

ALL THAT'S GOLD
DOES NOT GLITTER

I married my first date and high school sweetheart. As I walked down the aisle in the early '70s, a member of the "me" generation, I trembled under the burdensome prediction that the flame of passion, intimacy, and commitment would be extinguished in five to seven years.

Early in our marriage, I was on the lookout for suspicious signs signaling relationship deterioration. Many things troubled me, such as the simplicity of his love. He liked me—even in the presence of my weirdest quirks. Take, for example, the time I called to report hysterically that our new car was missing. For four hours he searched the parking area where I *knew* I'd left the car, before I remembered that I'd parked it in another lot.

His selective memory loss also puzzled me. He embraced my successes and passed on only my shining moments to our friends. Often I wondered how he could forget my mess-ups and appear blind to those mistakes he surely witnessed on a daily basis.

While some men specialize in romance, my husband specializes in humor. Etched vividly in my mind is one telephone call while we were dating. He announced that he had a surprise for me. My heart skipped a beat, thinking this must finally be the proposal I had already waited six years to receive.

When I saw his beaming face and the small box he carried, my hopes soared on the wings of encouragement. Closing my eyes, I waited with rapt anticipation for the "surprise" to be slipped on my finger. What I felt instead was a weight in my palm. My eyes popped open to gaze upon a purple turtle rock paperweight with two words painted on the cracks of its back: "Love Duane."

For the next year, I hinted and nudged him while drafting in my imagination the wildest romantic proposal scenario—a candle-light dinner out accompanied by violin music and him on bended knee. Part of my fantasy did come true. He proposed to me in a restaurant—Pogy's Pizza Palace! Music did play—recorded polka tunes that blared in the background.

It has been twenty-five years of a marriage that is not about perfection but instead a magical unfolding of love and laughter. Looking back, marriage met few of my earlier expectations. But once I followed Duane's example and let go of my unrealistic fantasies—just as he had—we fell perfectly in step.

Recently, I received from him a birthday card with the caption "With you, everything is fun." With so much history and material to play off of, the flame of passion and humor between us is alive and well. In fact, the longer we are together, the more golden our marriage becomes.

CANDIS FANCHER

*The truth of (her) origin is the birthright
of every (woman).*
FLORENCE ANNA FISHER

MOM, MY MOTHER, AND I

Before I even understood what it meant, my parents
told me I was adopted. At nineteen I read an Ann Lan-
ders column on adoption and fantasized about finding
my birth mother; but I wasn't sure if my curiosity would hurt
my adoptive parents, so I put it off. Not a day went by that I
didn't wonder who my birth mother was and why she'd given
me up.

Five years later, out of the blue, my mother asked, "Haven't
you ever been curious about your birth mother, or ever wanted
to find her?" Noticing my immediate interest, she gave me what
little information she had from the adoption process.

I spent weeks scouring through libraries, county recorders'
offices, courthouses, and phone books searching under my
mother's name at the time of adoption. The doctor who delivered me was tight-lipped; he'd only tell me that at the time of
birth my birth mother was in good health. After two months, I
came up empty-handed.

On the verge of setting aside my search, I met a birth mother
who'd successfully found the daughter she'd given up for adoption. April shared her story and pictures and suggested places I

hadn't looked. With renewed hope, I resumed my mission. As I dug up each new nugget of information, it led me to yet another. During weekly calls with April, I updated her on my finds and picked her brain for further ideas. I could see my destination, but felt as though I was slogging through a muddy creek bed to get there.

As the leads fizzled out one by one, April came up with the name of a friend who could look up marriage records. It turned out my birth mother had remarried, so her last name was different from the one I'd been searching under. Why hadn't I thought of that? I'd wasted so much time. April insisted we forget about that and get right back on the trail with our new lead.

The next evening, I sat cross-legged on my living room floor, sifting through a four-foot stack of old phone books. After an hour, my neck developed a golf ball–size knot, and my eyes wouldn't focus on the tiny print anymore.

The phone rang, and I jumped. Except for the leafing of pages, the room had been quiet.

"I found it!" April shouted on the other end. "It's a local number. You can call her right now!"

"Whoa . . . it's late," I said, fear creeping in. "Besides, what if it's not her?"

"Don't worry about that," April encouraged softly, "just dial."

After all these months of searching, I couldn't believe I needed more time. I washed my face, wrote down a few of the million questions I had, and decided to call in the morning. I dreamt of that call and woke every few hours and checked the clock before my mind fell back into cartwheels of conversation with my birth mother.

Sitting on the side of the bed early the next morning, I picked up the receiver. My palm was sweating against the plastic. I pushed half the numbers, then my nerves got the best of me, and I hung up.

I held on to the receiver, closed my eyes, and took a deep breath before I dialed again. A sleepy-voiced woman answered.

"Is this Joan?" I asked.

"Yes."

I asked her to jot down my name and number, then said, "Does September 27, 1962, mean anything to you?"

"Yes, it does."

My eyes filled with tears, and I leaned back against the pillows. "I think you're my birth mother."

Both crying, we spent the next twenty minutes describing ourselves. She told me I had a younger brother named Corey and an older one named Michael.

The following week, I brought Joan a small album filled with my baby and school pictures. We spent hours pouring over them. We held hands, reminisced, and forgot to go to the bathroom. When I summoned up the nerve to ask why she'd given me up, a tear slid down her cheek.

"I was already divorced and only twenty," she said. "Your older brother Michael was two. Just supporting him took all the energy and money I had. I wanted the best for you and knew I couldn't give it, so I let you go to people who could provide for you in ways I couldn't even imagine back then."

My stomach twisted. *How could Joan keep Michael and not me?* I thought. *I'd have been okay.* Yet I knew I wouldn't trade a day of growing up with the mom and dad who'd raised me.

Between the two of us, we went through the better part of a box of tissues in an afternoon and found joy in unexpected places. We discovered we're both photographers, pianists, vegetarians, and thrive on a goofy sense of humor.

When I told Mom I'd found Joan, she invited her to come share a lasagna supper with our family. In the living room before dinner, they sat on either side of me, two of the most generous women I know. I didn't know whose hand to squeeze. Mom patted my hand and nodded toward Joan. I turned to find Joan searching my every feature and realized how much we resembled each other, from the turn of the mouth to the shape of the brow. Mom's eyes started to mist over. Maybe she saw it too. All I saw was how lucky I was to be each woman's daughter and how, in their own separate ways, both love me dearly.

ROBIN MICHELLE SILK

PICTURE PERFECT

Sometimes *God shapes our lives in ways we don't quite realize.* When I was about nine years old, my father and I went to church together every Sunday. He met me after my Sunday school class, and together we took our place in the sanctuary of the Baptist church, fifth pew from the back. I always hoped we could make it to our seat without someone asking, "Where is your mother today?" or "Where is your wife today?" It bothered me that they put my father in such an uncomfortable spot. My mother never went to church. Everyone knew it. The very question seemed to prove my mother's point. She said church was full of hypocrites, people only presenting themselves as Christians but not really behaving as Christians.

Still, the other mothers didn't seem so terrible to me. They taught Sunday school, played the piano, brought potato salad to banquets, and helped with crafts at Bible School. My mother was a bookkeeper at a car dealership. She did our laundry on Saturday, sewed our clothes at night, and never drank anything stronger than Coca-Cola. And she never went to dances, unlike certain people she could name, but didn't, who belonged to the town's one country club. I wanted her to drink iced tea and sing in the choir.

Even though I was more accustomed to the company of adults than children, I still found it impossible to follow the specifics of the Sunday sermons. Instead, as I sat next to my father, I gazed at the photographs in my Sunday school quarterly or on the church bulletin and dreamed of a different life. I filled my fantasy with flowers in rich purples and sunny yellows, paths leading to green pastures, and pure white lilies. In this dream life, my mother kissed my father as he went off to work, put on her ruffled apron, and spent the day baking cookies and reading to me. I wanted whatever it was in real life to go away that unexpectedly caused one or both of my parents to slam the bedroom door, scream threats of divorce, throw our few plates against the wall, or speed away from the house with screeching tires.

Grown now, a wife and mother myself, I found myself one weekend at the cabin in the woods where my husband, Tom, and I retreat for weekends. All day the wind blew. In the setting sun, the dust-filled sky looked red and angry. Then the thunder rolled in. There was lightning and finally rain.

Standing at the kitchen sink after dinner with the window open, I let the rain mist my face. Pea-size hail peppered the deck and roof. Tom ran out to see if he had closed the pickup's windows. A light breeze seemed to come from every direction, forcing us to close all the windows. We stood on the deck in the first drops, smelling the rain and dust. Later I looked out the door, to the north, and the air had cleared. The red haze had disappeared and a mist in the hollows thickened and rose.

A screech owl flapped in the big oak tree, trying to hold his perch in the rising wind. He flew to a safer branch, missed, almost fell, grabbed the trunk, and climbed up, pulling himself with beak and claw to the crook of a branch. There he settled his wings and faced us. His gray fuzz fluffed out around him like a feathery aura. Occasionally he squeaked.

By bedtime the rain had stopped. We opened the windows. The house was warm and stuffy. The bedroom ceiling fan decided to make a loud humming, so we turned it off and settled in, covers tossed aside. In the night I heard the soft rain start up again and groggily decided it was okay to leave all the windows open. In the morning, Tom and I slept late, quilts pulled up against the cool spring breeze.

Lying in bed, we gazed out at the redbud in bloom, the trees in partial leaf against the gray sky, the purple ajuga shoots within the rock border outlining the circle drive and yellow iris bursting open at one end of the split log bench. Framed in the open window, the scene somehow looked familiar, and then I remembered those Sunday school pictures. Inside this magical springtime setting, I see a child's unspoken prayers, answered: to have this place, this time, this husband, our daughter, this life I never thought possible when I was that little girl dreaming through a Sunday sermon. And I understand, life is full of answered prayers, if I just take time to see.

CAROL NEWMAN

I was vegetarian
until I started leaning towards sunlight.
RITA RUDNER

DON'T BE GRUEL

Visions of low-fat, high-fiber, vitamin-rich foods entertained entire dinner fantasies in my head. I vowed to replace fried chicken and biscuits with newfound nourishing wonders to be poached, steamed, and lightly sautéed in a droplet of oil. I planned to chop, dice, mince, and roast my way through the holidays and create culinary converts.

My first endeavor would be bread. I could bake many loaves, freeze them for future dinners. In my Missouri hometown of Cape Girardeau, my mother's hairdresser, Shirley, said, "You know, I always keep a loaf of homemade bread froze up for company."

I would delight senses with fresh bread baking. I chose a recipe for gruel bread from a new vegetarian cookbook. It sounded pure and frugal, and incorporated the following ingredients: leftover vegetables, beans, cooked grains, and salads. I checked the refrigerator and found part of a can of tuna cat food. (We didn't have a cat, but sometimes strays dropped by for dinner.) I had plain yogurt, olives, onions, eggs, milk, and vinegar, but no leftovers suitable for my recipe. I started from scratch.

At the grocery store I purchased organic carrots, kale, potatoes, red peppers, broccoli, and cabbage. I was armed with fresh, soon-to-be-leftover vegetables. To my grocery store cart I added stone-ground wheat flour, sea salt, and olive oil from Tuscany.

At home, I steamed, pureed, and kneaded my wondrous mass until it glistened and stretched into shocking abundance. I oiled bread pans with a smidgen of oil, filled them with dough that I covered with checkered damp cotton towels. The bread flavored itself with all of those pureed broccoli stalks, onions, and beets.

My husband arrived home as the bread cooled. "What is that smell?"

"Gruel bread. I baked it for your supper, a meal in itself. No yeast or white sugar. It's all vegetables. Good for us."

"Good for whom? Gruel bread? Isn't that some thin porridge that the British serve up in those suffering stories you read? Do you have stone soup to go with it?"

My husband stopped laughing and teasing when the bread glued itself to the pans. I prodded and probed loaves into chunks, tried to slice it paper thin like the book said, and then we leaned over the kitchen sink and sampled pieces without saying a word. I left the kitchen to look up the word *gruel* in the dictionary. The second definition listed said: "Old British Collog. = punishment."

My husband sensed the seriousness of my silence. He said, "Hey, let's go out and try that new restaurant, Bandera's. They have chicken roasted on a spit." And then he sang, "Chestnuts roasting on an open fire . . ."

"Well, I guess we might as well go out to eat, but first will you bury the bread in the compost heap?" I smiled to myself when I remembered how compact semifrozen compost might be. His just due for teasing!

Two months elapsed. My grown son dropped his lab puppy, Bud, by the house for me to dog-sit. The dog was energized by his new space, and entertained himself by digging in the compost pile. Piece by piece he unearthed my gruel bread. I chased him and recovered the near-petrified mass and tossed it over the fence. He was dedicated to his task. I decided there was nothing harmful in the bread and let him continue to dig. He brought his treasure to the patio, secured his find between his front paws, and chewed and gnawed through the rest of the afternoon.

The following week Bud went to the veterinarian for his five-month checkup. My son reported, "The vet says Bud is very healthy and shows evidence of having excellent nutrition. He's lean and strong without an ounce of fat on him. His coat shines. He is alert and content."

"Wow!" I said. "Gruel bread! Let's market it as a high-fiber, vitamin-rich, low-fat snack for dogs. It can be stored in your winter compost pile. Like my mom's hairdresser, people can say, 'I have a snack froze up for any stray company or visiting pups!' "

JUDITH BADER JONES

FROM SUITS TO SWEATS

When I was growing up, my role model was Julie, the social director on the television show *Love Boat*. I dreamed of a career of sun, fun, swimming pools, and exercise—all on a great big cruise ship. It was a deep, dark, silent dream that didn't seem possible.

I proceeded on the usual route—never giving voice to my dream—spending ten years in advertising and sales after graduating from college. On one assignment, I supervised a commercial at a health spa and had a *Love Boat* moment. *I wish I could work in an environment like this, what an ideal job,* I thought, then shrugged it off and went about my business.

I worked in radio advertising in San Diego. As I made sales calls, I would hear a particular upbeat song on the radio and automatically create an aerobic routine in my head. I had a surprising ability to visualize each step. As work pressures mounted, my desire to move into the "fitness and fun" world grew.

My thirty-second birthday landed on a Friday, and that's the day my regular job and my dream job collided. I walked into my sales manager's office and struck a deal. I would quit, but first I would work short hours, service my existing clients, and use the rest of the time to search for a new job. In turn, he would have time to search for my replacement. I expected the job search to take up to two months.

Monday morning came, and I sat down with the phone book. I looked under "Health Clubs" in the Yellow Pages and started with Atlas Health Club. I had heard of its upscale reputation and it intrigued me. I made the call and hit pay dirt. The woman who answered informed me that the aerobics coordinator had broken her arm and they needed a replacement. As I waited for the coordinator to come on the line, I started to sweat—and I wasn't even working out! I put on my best enthusiastic aerobics animal persona and went in that day to try out. Afterward, she asked if I could start the next day. I looked at her in horror and said, "No, I'm rusty, and I need some music."

"If I work with you for the next couple of days, can you start Thursday?" she inquired.

"Yes." I beamed, and my career in fitness began. By Friday I had a second job teaching at the YMCA. The next week, I landed two more teaching positions. I was on my way; my dream was taking shape.

Just twenty miles north of San Diego was the Golden Door, one of the most exclusive spas in the world that catered to an elite clientele. My next goal was to work there. I calculated it would take me about two years. I enrolled at the University of California San Diego and began taking extension courses in anatomy and physiology to strengthen my credibility. I sent the Golden Door my résumé and repeatedly called the fitness supervisor to no avail. With each call, though, the secretary and I developed a friendly rapport.

Two weeks later, she called me. It seemed the supervisor was having a hard time finding a hostess to dine with guests and act as a backup in fitness. She wanted someone with personality. The secretary told her boss that I was the person for that job. Just what I wanted to hear!

I interviewed twice before the supervisor offered me a position. She explained that after two months I would be eligible to join the fitness staff full-time. But the best news was yet to come. After one year of employment, I would qualify to join the Spa at Sea program and work on the Cunard cruise ships. I imagine my expression closely paralleled that of someone who had just won the lottery! My *Love Boat* dream was becoming a reality.

And so what I thought would take two years took only two action-packed months. After a year's time, I flew to New York and boarded the *Queen Elizabeth II* for a four-month assignment. I didn't play "Julie" but I did play! It really was sun, fun, swimming pools, and exercise on a great big boat. When I walked up the ramp to board the ship, it felt like déjà vu. After all, I'd seen it all along.

BARBARA DALBEY

If anything can be sweeter than one's first love,
it must be that love recaptured.
AUTHOR UNKNOWN

FIRST LOVE, LASTING LOVE

I slid into the driver's seat, laid my head on the steering wheel, and sobbed. For a moment none of it seemed real: the solid strike of the judge's gavel; the clerk's final pronouncement: "You are now divorced." I never wanted to be a "divorced" woman, and after twenty-one years of marriage, our friends thought I was insane to leave. After all, my husband was the number one sales representative for a national company and, to all appearances, had personality plus. They didn't see the controlling, verbally abusive, unpredictable man I'd lived with over the years.

Following the divorce, my two teenagers and I eventually settled into a comfortable routine at home. Because my ex-husband had traveled extensively, his absence during the week didn't faze me, but come weekends I volunteered for overtime at work, called friends for dinner and movies, and worked the high school concession stand, anything to fill the void while my kids did "their thing." Work turned out to be a blessing, a constant in my life that kept me focused on something besides the flux in my personal life.

Several weeks after the divorce had been finalized, my employer sent me out of town on business to the same city where my first love lived. I hadn't seen Bud in twenty-five years and decided that as long as I was "cleaning house," I'd seek some closure with him, too. I set up a lunch.

To my surprise, Bud met me at the airport. Over lunch, we reminisced about our early relationship, the long separation during our engagement due to his military service, and the pain of ending our relationship the year after he returned from overseas. Over coffee I told him about my children, my work, and finally about my divorce. He shared pictures of his two young sons and quietly told me that he too was divorced. The afternoon stretched into evening and dinner with wine and more conversation. We met for lunch and dinner each day of my stay and promised to keep in touch.

No sooner did I step through the door at home than the phone rang. After a month of daily calls, I was on a plane to Bud again. Our first Christmas together was the kind of Christmas I thought possible only for other people. Bud presented me with the same engagement ring he had given me for Christmas in 1969.

Our wedding day dawned sunny and warm. Gathered in my oldest friend's living room were Bud's brothers with their wives and children, friends we had known for thirty years, and friends we had made over the years we'd been apart. When the minister asked each of our children if they had anything to say, my two told Bud they were glad we had found each other again and asked him to treat me kindly—to love me forever—because after all these years I deserved to be happy. Bud's little boys told me they were glad I was marrying Daddy and looked forward to my moving into their home.

Bud's vows took me by surprise: "Annie, from the first day I met you, I have known a truth . . . and that is the same truth that I know today. I love you for our yesterdays, for today, and for all of our tomorrows."

During my vows, I felt myself trembling as if I were cold, but I'd never felt such warmth as I did standing with Bud, hand in hand. "Bud, I fell in love with you when I was eighteen years old, and here I stand thirty years later, in love with you still. You make me laugh . . . you make me feel treasured . . . you were my first love and you will be my last . . . and so today, in the presence of our family and friends, I give you my heart and love, knowing that it will be well cared for."

Surrounded by our children and my son-in-law, we lit a unity candle with seven wicks—one for each of us. Smoke from the candle floated upward, and the Hallelujah Chorus filled the room as the minister pronounced us man and wife. I'd always dreamed of this moment, never once believing it would come true.

I am convinced that God intervened in our lives and provided a second chance for us to come together. I am a new person in this love. I make time to tell those close to me I love them. I listen with a new perspective to people who trust and confide in me. I'm more empathetic to the pain of others. I laugh more and worry less.

After a year of married life, Bud still takes my breath away as he walks through the door at the end of a busy day. Each night, as his good-night kiss lingers, I thank God for the courage it took to listen to my empty heart and give it all the love it desired.

ANNIE WILSON

IN GOD'S TIMING

Richard and I slipped into the crowded room, our hands tightly clasped. We picked up an information packet and application form, then found two seats near the front.

I glanced around the room. Were these people as nervous as I felt? Had they waited for a child as long as we had?

After ten years of trying to get pregnant, a devastating false pregnancy, and years of infertility tests and treatments, we were starting the adoption process. I didn't feel as if it was the end of a struggle, but instead a new beginning.

I had finally given my barrenness to God, along with the pain and regret. Having a family was what was important to us, not how we became a family.

Over the years we solicited information on many agencies. Our teacher's and writer's incomes did not meet the requirements of some, and the long years of waiting did not appeal to us. We had already waited so long.

When we watched our friends adopt two wonderful children through the Department of Human Services, we knew this was our chance.

There were no guarantees. We would have to attend ten weeks of parenting classes, fill out extensive paperwork, open our lives to scrutiny, and be flexible in the age and background of the child we would be willing to accept.

Once the orientation was over, our next step was to fill out an application and wait for an invitation to the classes. On March

11, 1991, we began what was to be months of learning and preparing, emotional ups and downs, and times of wondering if we were doing the right thing.

In spite of all that lay ahead, we were excited and hopeful. For the first time in years, I couldn't wait to look around the children's section in a department store. We talked about how things would be so different through the eyes of a child. Our child.

Our first hurdle was a stack of paperwork the size of a small phone book. We learned more about ourselves than we'd ever known.

The weekly classes were two hours of learning about the children of abuse, neglect, or abandonment—and about ourselves. Role-playing put us in the children's world, in their parents' places, and in the places of the caseworkers, often caught in the middle.

We knew that somewhere a child waited for us, and we prayed for its safety. At times, I felt guilty. I knew that as we anticipated there would be a child for us at the end of our classes and home visits, these children were coming from broken homes. Was my desire for a child so strong that I hoped for such a thing to happen? I prayed and listened to God and my heart, and came to understand the sad truth that not all parents are able to properly care for the children they were blessed with. Through long years of desire to raise a child of our own, we were being prepared to give a home to a youngster who needed a safe and healthy environment.

One by one, we completed the list of projects we were given. Sometimes, we were overwhelmed with the information and by the decisions we had to make. At times, we left the meetings excited, talking for hours. Other times, we felt burdened by the responsibility. Even more, I was afraid that for some reason we would be turned down.

The stress and hard work seemed to draw Richard and me

closer. I marveled at what a wonderful father our child would have. I watched him in different ways and saw that he was kind, considerate, thoughtful, and caring.

After our first home visit, we felt as if we could float around the house. Our caseworker was impressed with our marriage and what had been said about us from our references. When she left, after weeks of feeling "if we adopt," it suddenly felt more like *"when."*

Before we knew it, the classes were over. We were anxious for our caseworker to finish our personal interviews.

I began preparing the extra room. I painted and cleaned, carefully arranging stuffed animals around the floor. By the first of July everything had been completed, and we'd been approved. We prepared ourselves for the most difficult part.

Waiting.

Whenever the phone rang, my heart skipped a beat. We called our answering machine constantly when we were away.

But soon the summer came to an end and our extra room was still empty. I spent time in our child's room, trying to be patient.

The old bitterness over our childlessness crept back in. The waiting seemed to last forever. I prayed for peace.

A few days later, I passed a church. The marquis shone in the night: DO WE MISTAKE GOD'S PATIENCE FOR ABSENCE?

My eyes filled with tears. Yes, I had wondered if God was ignoring us. The peace I had prayed for seeped inside me, and I felt hope once again.

On Monday, November 4, at 2:30 P.M., the phone rang. "Kathy, is there something you've been wanting for Christmas?" our caseworker asked.

I gripped the phone. "Yes."

Teasingly, she prodded, "And what might that be?"

The words came out in a rush. "A child!"

"Well, I think we have some great news for you."

Suddenly the waiting was over. Our eight-and-a-half-month-old daughter was waiting for us, so much younger than we'd even dared to hope for.

But God wasn't finished letting us know how he had heard our prayers. When Richard and I were dating, we chose the name Michael or Michelle for our first child.

Our new daughter's middle name was Michelle, the name her foster parents had called her since she came to them at three days old.

Our daughter was our child in so many ways.

As I look at my sweet child, now approaching her eighth birthday, I think of how I had worried and fretted, even gave up hope, then saw it reborn in her eyes.

When others see our daughter, they speak of how lucky she is to have parents who love her. But I tell them that *we* are the lucky ones—to have had our prayers answered with a miracle we call Michelle.

KATHRYN LAY

VI

ONE STEP AT A TIME

The light you carry may illuminate only one step at a time, but as you move forward the next step will be revealed.

MARY MANIN MORRISSEY

THE QUEEN-SIZE BED

*L*ast summer, while living in New York City, I decided to take a solo driving trip that ended up being a
10,000-mile circle around the United States. Never in my
life had I attempted anything that momentous alone, but it
seemed I had been forever mired in the painful dissolution of my
six-year marriage. There's nothing like prolonged agony to make
you desirous of a new perspective. I needed a break, some time
away to not think so much. If I was lucky, maybe I could again
begin to trust. After all, I was heading out alone into the great
open Universe.

I had no particular agenda, just a direction . . . west. Scattered
all across the country were friends I looked forward to visiting
should I make it to where they were. A couple of these friends
had provided me with the only other potential event penciled
into this free-form schedule—a blind date—that is, if I made it to
Portland, Oregon.

Several weeks later (although it felt like a time warp), I called a
complete stranger to say I was heading his way. I stood at a bank
of pay phones outside Backpacker's Heaven in Glacier, Montana,
and had a surprisingly pleasant conversation with a man I was
beginning to feel I was destined to meet.

From Seattle, I called to say I was getting closer. By then we
had enjoyed several phone conversations; and although I no
longer considered him a complete stranger, he was still a blind
date.

"What do you look like?" I asked.

"What do I look like?" he repeated, and I realized he wasn't that accustomed to looking at or describing himself. I took this to be a good sign.

"I'm about six-foot-two, a hundred and ninety-five pounds, and have a receding hairline and blue-gray eyes."

He was several years younger than me, which was a first, but I rather thought I would enjoy tapping into that "older woman" mystique.

"Do you like sushi? I know this great place where we can eat sushi and watch sumo wrestling from Japan via satellite. Maybe we should meet at the restaurant? By the way, you're more than welcome to stay at my house. I have a guest room."

His house was a cabin at the base of Mount Hood, some seventy miles outside of Portland.

"Thank you, but I'll get a hotel room. I like sushi. The jury is still out on sumo. So what's the deal, how do we meet?" I asked.

"I tell you what, you get to Portland, let me know where you're staying and I'll come get you," he answered.

I called to make a reservation at the Mallory Hotel, specifically requesting a single bed. I hadn't sworn off men, but I realized that being married for six years to a man who now believes he's gay had taken the wind out of my sails, not to mention giving me a feeling of complete rejection as a sexual being. To say I had notions of inadequacy dancing through my psyche is being less than candid.

I arrived at the Mallory to discover that because of a computer glitch my personal room key allowed entrance to a room with a queen-size bed instead of the single bed requested. I still hadn't met this man. Two hours and counting, so I took a nap, careful to lie on both sides of my head so my hair would flatten in stereo.

I tried hard not to have expectations or to be nervous. Down in the lobby, I sampled different chairs and vantage points, finally settling for a cushy green velveteen perch. I brought my book along, like I actually thought I would read. I strategically placed myself so that he could easily see me when he reached the top step and then crossed and uncrossed my legs trying to determine which was the most appropriate cross to convey a casual, confident nonchalance . . . and read page 115 one more time.

To enter the Mallory on the street level requires a climb of eight or nine steps to arrive in the lobby. It was like slowly unwrapping a present. First, I could see the top of his head, then the face, with the whole of a person revealed in eight-inch increments until he reached the last step. I noticed the receding hairline first and knew instantly it was him, my blind date. From somewhere in my gut, I reevaluated my self-imposed stance on celibacy. All my casual nonchalance blew out the window as I hurried across the lobby.

"Are you by any chance looking for Myra?" I said to the good-looking, tall man who had just reached the top of the stairs.

"Hi, sorry I'm late," he replied. He smiled.

We were both starving and started walking across town, headed for sushi and sumo. We did the gentlemanly two-step across town, as I was repositioned on the inside of him whenever necessity demanded. I was charmed by his chivalry.

During dinner, there was no lull in conversation, and initially, when our eyes met, we both blushed and looked away. Whether or not I consumed food soon ceased to be an issue. We sipped wine and laughed a lot.

Tension increased, and toward the end of the meal it was so thick between us that I felt certain it was visible, like an aura. I was sure that everyone in the restaurant could see these hot, red flames dancing around us that spoke of possibilities I had long since lost hope in. Maybe life does imitate art, or sport—or, on this night, sumo. We watched the TV monitors as two massive, half-naked bodies stalked around each other and then with some unspoken communication slammed into each other, wrestled there, and backed away.

For whatever reason, it became impossible, when our eyes met, to do anything but lock in and stay engaged as long as we dared. It felt as though our waitress, had she happened by in one of those profoundly intimate moments, would have been able to actually see what I only felt. She would have known what I looked like in my skinny body with no tan lines. She would have seen my yearning as big as the past six years. I felt my soul was on display in the guise of something raw, something akin to power.

We began to meander toward the river, all the while talking and all the while feeling our bodies brush against each other. Our mutual restraint only added to the tension. Feeling awkward, I fell into the conversational babble mode. He didn't say much, just backed me up against the railing above the river and asked to kiss me.

"Yes," I answered.

He bent down and very sweetly put his lips to mine in a tender, well-mannered kiss that seemed to say "I don't want to come on too strong." I returned same, hoping that I was communicating that he needn't always be such a gentleman.

Once again, we began a slow hand-in-hand amble back to the hotel. A few more blocks and I would have to settle this struggle between my head, my upbringing, my heart, and my urgency. He had offered to get another hotel room, said this was my call, and would I be interested in going to the Oregon coast the next day. I began to remember why I had embarked on this trip. About not thinking and trusting the fact that I believe everything happens for a reason. Why had I, after all, wound up with a bed for two when I requested a bed for one? I told him about the *accidental* big bed and invited him to stay the night. Our amble picked up pace.

Five days later, traveling solo again, I pulled away from his log cabin at the base of Mount Hood and was brought to tears by the beauty around me. I cried out of gratitude for the genius of the Universe to have created something so perfect. For the journey into trust that had guided me all the way to Oregon and for that same genius that knew, better than me, how badly I needed that queen-size bed.

MYRA WINNER

DISCOVERING
MY SPECIAL DELIVERY

I became a mail carrier solely through a series of accidents. At work I became friends with the carrier who brought the mail to the mailroom. Aware of how hard I struggled to survive on little more than minimum wage during a time of double-digit inflation, he told me when the post office started hiring. When self-doubt made me hesitate, he threatened to kick the butt of my well-patched jeans all the way down to the personnel office.

I swallowed my fear and put in an application. To my surprise, I was hired as a mail handler and was later told that I was the first woman in Denver assigned full dock duties. All I cared about at the time was that I had a steady job with good pay, sick leave, health insurance, and a retirement plan. Now I'd even have the chance to buy a house.

After I proved myself on the dock, I managed to secure a route as a substitute mail carrier in one of the roughest neighborhoods in Denver. Women were still rare as mail carriers, and this was the only station willing to give me a chance. As a kid, I grew up the tagalong girl in a tough neighborhood commanded by boys. Membership in the gang was contingent upon athletic ability, and I was a sickly, uncoordinated girl, unsuited to play any position beside backstop at baseball games. I longed to be "one of the guys" but always found myself on the outside looking in.

I was an outsider in my family, too. My parents dreamed I

would rise beyond their hand-to-mouth existence. They dreamed I'd be a pretty, demure, feminine girl with an upwardly mobile husband. They pictured me in a solid career as a veterinarian, CPA, or museum curator. Something indoors, safe and respectable. I wasn't any of those things, but carrying mail, I found myself at home in my own skin for the first time in my life.

The post office provided the perfect environment for me. What I couldn't do by brute force I learned to finesse. The more I proved I was willing to do the job and not ask for special favors, the more the other carriers warmed up to me.

I worked with people who were a wonderful combination of caring, brains, honesty, and playful rowdiness. I learned there was the right way to do the job and there was the management's way. We took pride in going by the rules—right by them—to get the job done.

Instead of being passed over because I wasn't pretty, I got raises because I put in my time and did the job. Pretty didn't matter when I had to step over a passed-out drunk to make a delivery. Demure didn't cut it when I was delivering to pimps, prostitutes, drug dealers, and the legally insane. Feminine wasn't relevant when the guy I was talking to one day was murdered the next. Somehow, I knew when to be courteous, when to launch a full verbal assault, or when to just lie low.

I bid for the station closest to home, and four years later got a route with my kind of people—hardworking, middle income, young families, and the elderly. I found a sense of community. I fit in both at the station and out on the route. Still, I thought I wanted more. I went to school, got a real estate license, became an accredited financial planner, and kept carrying mail.

When I didn't change jobs after I acquired new skills, I thought something was wrong with me. Was I afraid to succeed? Was I afraid to fail? After much soul-searching, I realized I didn't leave because I love what I do. I pursued other careers to please my parents. I discovered I was surrounded by acceptance at work, the kind I could never earn from my folks. I chose what I loved over what others expected and found peace of mind.

One day, Connor, a five-year-old boy on my route, reinforced my belief that I had made the right decision. He had just joined a T-ball team and was trying to practice by himself. His front walk had a mild slope, so he rolled the ball down a way, ran to the bottom, and caught the ball at the end. Needless to say, it didn't provide much of a challenge. After warning him about windows, I showed him how to throw the ball against the house and catch it when it bounced off. He was delighted! He asked me if I played T-ball when I was little. I explained that they didn't have T-ball back then and that they wouldn't have let girls play anyway. That puzzled him and he asked me why. Not wanting to confuse him with the politics of the issue, I just told him that they thought girls probably wouldn't be interested. He pondered that for a minute and then looked up at me shyly out of the corner of his eye and said, "But they were wrong, weren't they?"

Oh, the power I found in that statement! How many times I've stifled my true self to mold my life to the expectations of others. Equestrians have a saying that deals with the fear of falling off: "Throw your heart over the fence and your horse will follow."

DEBRA SMITH

BOOTS, BACKS, AND BILLS

We were drinking our Sunday morning coffee and reading the paper when my husband suggested I get a job.

"Be helpful with bills," he said.

"But who will sing to the plants, put out the cat, lick the stamps on the bills, pay the postage due, watch *The Young and the Restless* on television, read the morning news, and talk on the phone?"

My husband stopped smiling. He had on his serious face. I reconsidered.

"I'll need to spruce up my wardrobe with a new outfit and get a permanent for interviews."

He nodded approval.

I bought a long flared wool skirt and a linen blouse. My hair was clipped and curled. The boots came last. They were black leather with slender high heels and priced at one hundred and fifty-nine dollars. I entered that amount in my checkbook under "groceries."

The following day I looked for a job. I felt well groomed. Eyes met mine briefly and then looked down to admire my feet as I tapped over concrete walks, clicking wonderfully on tiled floors of office buildings.

Eight hours later, I shed my finery and crawled into my warm waterbed. I smiled my last "Mona Lisa" smile.

Morning sunlight and throes of low back pain awakened me. Getting out of bed was a monumental task. Yesterday's confident legs straddled the waterbed frame to maneuver my feet to the floor. The water in our bed swished and rolled as pain trouped across my lumbar sacral region, down my leg, and back again.

I shuffled to the kitchen in brown scuffs. Standing was bearable, but sitting was being a robot molded and flexed into one position and riveted to a chair.

An ice pack and I retired for the next two days. On the third day I called the doctor.

The doctor listened to my boot story. He mumbled something about vanity and prescribed pills to relax muscles, the skeletal ones that were moving like Mexican jumping beans.

"Put a board under your mattress," the doctor advised.

My husband refused to put a board under our waterbed mattress. He moved me to a twin bed in a room at the back of the house, a room with Legos, comics, and seven-year-olds. I was demoted. The sounds of the laughing family members wandered back to me as I adjusted my ice pack and read another mystery.

The dishes mused in the sink. The cat washed a few. The kids argued over the last clean tube sock, their father's. I kept remembering that song, "These Boots Are Made for Walking."

X rays followed. No damage, only muscle spasms. Still in pain, I sat with discomfort in the family room. I was wearing a pair of five-year-old flat shoes. My seven-year-old studied my feet and said, "Mom, aren't you ever going to outgrow those shoes?" I laughed in spite of pain.

I made out the following list and handed it to my husband.

Boots: One hundred and fifty-nine dollars
Medicine: Thirty-five dollars
X rays: One hundred and fifty dollars
Blouse: Thirty-five dollars
Permanent: Sixty-five dollars
Doctor: Eighty dollars

TV Dinners: Twenty dollars
Grand Total: Five hundred and forty-four dollars

I picked up the classified section of the paper. "Oh, look, honey, maybe I could apply for this one!"

My husband touched my hand and said, "But who would sing to the cat and put out the plants?"

JUDITH BADER JONES

. . . I've made it a rule to pull in my stomach
and let my behind look after itself.
AGATHA CHRISTIE

THE ROAD LEADING
TO SPANDEX

I've always felt out of sync with the times—as a girl I'd shinny up a tree after my brother, but my mother would stand at the bottom, red in the face, and holler, "Get down here right this minute." I'd have to slide down, go inside, bathe, and sit rocking on the porch for the rest of the evening staring into my black patent leather shoes. As a teenager, the '50s styles dictated that I should cover my slim body with a circular felt poodle skirt down to my thick white bobby socks and on top wear an Eisenhower jacket that would have fit Eisenhower.

Many years later, in the dimness of my bedroom, the only signs of aging I paid much attention to were my underarms, which resembled crepe paper, and a tendency to put on a few pounds, both of which I hid under yawning jeans and T-shirts.

One morning, however, when my jeans belched instead of yawning, I decided to investigate the brand-new fitness facility in a nearby shopping center. I should have been warned by the glaring lights and pulsating music that my illusions were about to be shattered. Before me in a room encased in mirrors and dominated by a giant trapezoidal steel gym set, nubile girls, harlequins in shimmering body suits, performed a mechanized ballet upon its pulleys. Silver weights clanked and steel shafts rose and fell in perfect synchronization. Along the sides of the room, other slim young women worked on brown Naugahyde spot-reducing machines resembling surreal dental chairs. Still others, graceful as irises, stretched their slender legs on ballet bars.

I was so entranced by the scene that I didn't notice a nymphet in an iridescent "diaper" until she bounced up to me, shook my hand vigorously, and said, "I'm Olga, the director." While appraising her sinewy thighs enviously, I explained that I felt a few sit-ups would take care of the fat roll I had developed around my middle. She smiled pensively and said, "Let's take a tour of the building, then I'll get your weight and measurements, compare those with the national fitness standards, and see where you stand."

Back in her office, Olga removed a tape measure from her bracelet-size waist and stretched it around mine. Then she weighed me. The scale undulated wearily. Olga was standing so close we exchanged breaths. She saddled the 100-pound puck on the bridge, and with the tip of her pencil teased the upper measure past all of my favorite numbers. The balance arrow stayed stubbornly up. When it started downward we both sighed with relief. Then she called "Alicia" to a girl who was lifting weights across the room. Alicia bounded over, her skin glowing from the recent exercise. When I was young, I could have lifted heavier weights than Alicia, but I wasn't allowed to.

"I won't have to use those things, will I?" I said, pointing to the weights.

Alicia swung her ponytail from side to side. "Well, maybe later, but for someone your age, we usually start with twenty minutes of rapid walking on the treadmill and then sets of weight-lifting repetitions on our machines."

Someone my age smiled and said I hoped it wouldn't take too long.

Alicia instructed me on several machines designed like medieval torture instruments. Then we progressed to the pectoral crunch—the self-abasing Puritans must have invented this one just before the stocks.

"This will take care of those hanging places," she said, pinching my delicate underarms. I wedged myself into the crunch. In the mirror I noticed for the first time that when I sat down, my midriff dissolved into a mud slide.

"Okay. You'll do this twenty times," she said. "Just put your hands behind these flaps and push in until they meet over your nose. I'll be right back." I put my arms behind the flaps and attempted to bring them forward. The only change I noticed was that my underarm jelly quivered even more.

Next she took me to the treadmill and started it slowly. I watched the little old lady next to me. She was a monochromatic study as she attempted to keep up with the relentlessly forward-moving belt. Her gray warm-up suit matched her hair. We smiled at each other in the mirror. I huffed and almost ran to keep up with the pace Alicia had set, then shifted down to a slower speed. *Five minutes is enough for the first day,* I thought, as I stopped the machine and sat on a bench. Twenty minutes later that lady slowed her belt to a stop. I resisted the impulse to help her off. She wiped sweat from her forehead and started the treadmill back up. As I struggled to work the leg lift, she came up beside me and said, "I took your program card by mistake—it's identical with mine."

As I gazed around the kaleidoscope of color accenting lithe bodies and listened to the music screeching, I understood how my mother felt that long-ago July day when I opened her bedroom door by mistake and saw her on her exercise mat, eyes bulged out with the effort of sit-ups—girdle off and midriff looking like unbaked sourdough bread. I made the mistake of giggling. "Close the door," she shouted hoarsely. "Someday you'll be sorry."

I was sorry. I was lying on the floor thinking about this when Alicia sprinted by. "Mrs. J., are you ready for aerobics? It will really help you with that reduced lung capacity." I went to the aerobics room and took my place in the back of the room. I whispered a question to the sufferer next to me. I didn't realize Alicia heard until she turned to me and said, "Yes, Mrs. J., I do know CPR, but we haven't even started yet."

After the warm-up, the music shifted into a psychotic frenzy as we pogoed in place. I felt my heart popping out of my body as I jiggled up and down in boxer shorts and an old Optimist T-shirt. The floor vibrated with the force of our running. The mirror shimmied as if it were a lake, but when I told Alicia my heart rate, she said I could work a little harder next time.

During the next few months, I went to the fitness center three times a week despite my body's twanging protest, then one day I awoke actually yearning to go. I felt alive and could bend over without pain for the first time in years. Decked out in spandex, I now approached the machines almost like a cowgirl in charge of her wild horse. I slung my leg over the duo squat and said, "Let's go for it, pardner." One day I was rotating the torso turn when a woman next to me said, "Isn't this hell on earth?" Before I could check myself, I said, "But think how gorgeous we're going to be." I realized I was having fun. I was beginning to find my waistline again and felt stronger every day.

One day three months later, Alicia didn't show up for aerobics, and I noticed a familiar figure at the front of the room. It was . . . my mouth dropped open . . . the little old lady in tennis shoes took her place before us. She pulled her jacket off, revealing a shapely body, turned, and beckoned to me.

"Janice, will you show the group the stretching exercises?" she said to me. "You do them so well. I've been watching your progress. Why, you're so trim, and you just glow."

She blew a little whistle, the music started, and she clapped her hands over her head, while running in place. "Okay, girls, let's go!" she yelled.

And I followed, my body perfectly in sync.

JANICE NORMAN

A CLEANSING
2000 STYLE

My son, Tyler, is six years old now and has grown beyond my protective shield. From his schoolmates, day-care buddies, and media exposure outside the home, he is learning colorful new phrases.

One day a friend of his came to play and educated my son on the fine art of insulting. From the front yard I could hear Tyler, who was playing on the backyard swings with his buddy, yell at the top of his lungs, "You couldn't find your wiener if it was attached to a hot dog bun!" Unfortunately, our backyard is situated in a good echo zone, so it was heard around the neighborhood. I was mortified.

Soon after, I woke up to hear my young boy referring to his little sister as a "butt." I shudder every time I hear that word because I think of the first and only time I used it. I was about my son's age when I heard it at school. Not knowing what it meant, I immediately tried it out on my mom when I got home from school. It's been twenty-six years and I still haven't forgotten the mouth washing I received.

Reflecting on that memory, I finally decided that it was time to take action. I had been threatening Tyler for months. I got out of bed and called him into the bathroom. When he realized what I meant to do, he had a look of utter disbelief on his face. He struggled valiantly, and I barely managed to get a dab of liquid hand soap in his mouth. This was *not* the way I remembered it happening to me! I was too scared of my mom to put up a fight, and the horror of a whole bar of soap in my mouth has scarred me forever. Tyler was not only *not* traumatized, he barely had anything to spit out! *Failed attempt,* I thought to myself.

And it was. Two days later we had another occurrence of the "butt" word. I was putting him to bed.

"Good night," I said.

"I love you," he replied. "When it's dark outside and all the stars are out, that's how much I love you."

Deeply touched by this sweetest declaration of love I've ever received from my son, I went into my bedroom to record this precious moment in the journal I write for him. Minutes later I overheard him talking to himself while in bed. "Kiss my butt," he said to no one in particular. He said it again, louder, enjoying the way it rolled off his tongue, "Kiss my b-u-t-t!"

Precious moment quickly forgotten, I once again called him into the bathroom. This time he was ready. I grabbed the first thing my hand touched, a bottle of shampoo. Again, as he struggled fiercely, using every ounce of his sixty-five-pound, four-foot-three-inch frame (my son is a very big six-year-old), I managed to reach one soapy finger into his mouth. Immediately, he started gagging, spitting, crying, and yelling. Now, *this* was serious. I would have done my mom proud. This time he was going to learn a lesson. He continued fussing dramatically and refused water because he didn't want the soap bubbling in his mouth. He started to gag some more. Knowing that he can make himself throw up by coughing, I told him to lean over the toilet, just in case. But he didn't vomit. Then, suddenly, he did. All over the bathroom floor. Cleaning up the mess, I decided I'd learned my lesson: what worked in the '60s doesn't necessarily work the same way in the new millennium.

Later, hugging and holding him, I repeated the words he told me earlier: "I love you as much as there are stars in the sky."

"I love you more," he said simply.

MELANIE ANDERSON-CASTER

All your dreams can come true . . .
if you have the courage to pursue them.
AUTHOR UNKNOWN

A STUDY IN CHARACTER

The job of a lifetime, that's what it was, secretary for the district attorney. I couldn't wait for my interview the next afternoon. This kind of position is what I've dreamed of, what all those years of college and entry level positions were for.

That night, I spent two hours going through my closet to pick out just the right outfit. What would I say to him? I curled up into my pillowy bed and stared at the ceiling, unable to sleep. How should I act? Nervous, I shut my eyes and tried to get some rest, but I kept tossing and turning.

Finally, the alarm clock woke me. I tried to open my eyes but something was wrong. My face felt stiff, strange. My hands flew to my cheeks.

"No!" My lips were unable to open all the way.

I ran to the bathroom and looked at myself in the bathroom mirror, horrified. My face was contorted like a stroke victim's. My eyes were misaligned. I couldn't move the right side of my face. I could barely recognize myself. What was happening to me? What nightmare did I wake up into?

My mother came into the room. "What's wrong?" Her eyes bulged as she withdrew in terror.

"What's happening to me?" I slurred to her.

"I'll take you to the emergency room," she finally gasped.

We were rushed in. The nurse took one look at me and called in a specialist. There, under the blazing white lights, my mother and I waited.

After several hours of tests, the doctor finally explained, "You have Bell's palsy. It is a condition in which your face muscles tighten because of stress. You need to get plenty of sleep, and in a few days your face will return to normal."

"But I have a job interview this afternoon," I sadly remembered.

"I'm sorry," the doctor said, concerned. "You should reschedule, maybe for later in the week."

During the long car ride home, all I could think about was how bad it would look to reschedule. Certainly, that would dampen my chances. Nobody reschedules with the district attorney. All the other applicants would have the advantage then, I concluded.

I looked at my watch and made the decision. "Mom, drop me off on Jacob Street. I'm going to the interview."

"Honey, I don't think you should. You look . . . strange," she said ever so gently.

I knew she was right. He probably would take one look at me and judge me by my appearance rather than by my experience and talent. I probably shouldn't go. But if I didn't, I'd always wonder if I could have gotten my dream job.

"No, Mom, take me there."

Reluctantly, she took me where I wanted to go. I walked right into the formidable office with the mahogany furniture and pillars of white marble, not letting my own self-consciousness or any disease stop me. Not now, not when I had worked so hard for so long to be given this opportunity.

I went to the woman sitting behind the front desk and said, as well as I could, "Nicole Jenkins to see Mr. Robertson."

She stared at my face. "He's expecting you. Go right in."

I entered the room to her right and saw a gray-haired man sitting behind the large desk reading a file.

Suddenly my nerves got the best of me and I had to sit. I took the chair in front of him.

"Hello," he said. "Miss Jenkins?"

"Yes. Please excuse me. I'm having a Bell's palsy attack. My doctor explained to me that it would last a few days. I came right from the hospital."

"You're very dedicated to come when you're not feeling up to speed," he responded after a pause.

"Yes, sir."

He spent a few minutes looking over my application. "Is everything on here correct?" He held it out to me.

I glanced over the paper. "Yes, but I failed to mention I type seventy-five words a minute."

"Wonderful." He smiled. "Out of one hundred points, you had our highest score on the application test. You scored well above average on grammar and computer programs."

"It comes easy for me," I honestly replied.

"Well, you are certainly qualified. You have an impressive background with related experience. I see here you worked for the navy."

"Directly with Legal Affairs," I said.

"When are you available?"

"Two weeks."

He gazed down onto his desk calendar. "The twenty-seventh then, be here at nine A.M."

I gasped. "You're hiring me?"

"Yes, you're perfect for the position."

I stood. "Thank you for believing in me. I won't let you down."

"I know." He smiled, rising from his desk to shake my hand. "Not only have you got the skills I'm looking for, you also have the character."

NIKKI JENKINS

GONE FISHIN'

*F*rightening words fell from my husband's lips one summer morning: "Why don't you go fishing with me this weekend?"

Over thirty years before, he had spoken these same words with disastrous consequences for me. How well I remembered stumbling over rough terrain, retrieving fish hooks from tree branches, and crawly things making welts on nearly every part of my body. I'd vowed never to go near a river again, with or without a rod and reel.

But I was loath to turn aside this earnest invitation from one with whom I planned to spend my rapidly approaching sunset years. "Good idea," I said, masking my apprehension. "When do we leave?"

Within two hours our fishing gear and overnight bags were in the back of our station wagon. By late afternoon we'd driven the considerable distance to a small town near my husband's favorite fishing grounds. We found a motel and had dinner at a local café.

Just after dessert, a feeling of dread overtook me. I had suddenly remembered that, in addition to the things already in my bank of unpleasant fishing memories, there were also bulls and an occasional snake.

But there sat my husband, smiling, oblivious to my true feelings and eager to share with me a very special part of his life. I knew I must face the inevitable. I was going river fishing and would somehow have to survive.

In the darkness of our motel room, panic set in. I slept for only brief periods, interrupted by horrible nightmares. Just as exhaustion brought merciful oblivion, an abrasive sound split the air. Our travel alarm had summoned my husband to his feet, and he cheerfully announced, "Time to hit the deck." He didn't seem to notice my red, swollen eyes, nor the pallor of my skin. We'd have a substantial breakfast and be on the river by sunrise.

After our meal, we headed the station wagon down narrow, graveled roads, which seemed to wind interminably through the darkness. Gradually a flush of pink along the horizon began to reveal the contours of grassy hillsides. My husband stopped the car on an old wooden bridge. "There she is!" he exclaimed with real affection in his voice. I allowed myself to look. Below ran dark water from which rose misty clouds of vapor. In the half-light, overhanging branches took on shapes that piqued my imagination. I was not reassured.

As we drove farther, the sun rose and I could see the pleasant, rolling countryside through which we traveled. By the time we found a suitable place to park the wagon, I had arrived at a certain state of compatibility with the landscape.

Still some distance from the river, we made our preparations. I was equipped with a carpenter's apron containing a jar of catfish bait, extra hooks, sinkers, and a pair of pliers. A rod and reel were placed in my right hand and a creel was hung over my left shoulder. I was now completely resigned.

Together we crossed a barbed-wire fence and tramped through a well-grazed meadow toward the water. I experienced a surprising moment of relief at my first glimpse of the river in broad daylight. Winding between grassy banks dotted with wildflowers, it reflected the blue of the summer sky and sparkled in the sun like thousands of tiny diamonds. My fears were somewhat eased.

I was given numerous instructions and shown a likely place to drop bait. I took the jar from my apron and removed the lid. Time had dulled my memory of the odor that now assailed my nostrils. Once again, I resisted the urge to retreat and forced myself to face the task at hand. I rolled some of the pungent mixture between my palms until it formed a small, smooth ball, pushed the dark brown sphere firmly over the three-pronged hook, and dropped the hook into the selected spot.

Reasonably satisfied that I could now manage on my own, my husband waded across the river to fish the opposite bank. The anxiety I felt at his departure was short-lived. A soft tugging had caused a tiny bounce at the end of my rod and all else ceased to matter.

The tugging grew stronger and the reel began to spin as the fish headed for a pile of brush downstream. "Stop him!" shouted my husband. My thumb finally found the trigger on the automatic reel, enabling me to shorten the line. Then, summoning all the strength in my rather small body, I gave a mighty heave and three pounds of channel catfish flew through the air. The shouting from the other side of the river grew louder. "I said stop him, not send him to the moon!" I scarcely recall the ensuing moments, but somehow the fish got landed.

I was ecstatic! Never mind that I might have lost my prize had he not swallowed the hook or that I had a slight twinge of regret for having removed a creature from his native habitat. Never mind that a herd of cattle now peered at us from the brink of a hill and one member of the group looked suspiciously like a bull. I was as happy as a child at Christmas!

That day, I learned to endure minor hardships in order to reap large rewards. I was privileged to watch a doe and fawn graze on the other side of the river. A great blue heron skimmed the water in search of a meal, a beaver gnawed at a fallen tree, squirrels chased one another, and birds communicated from the treetops. At times there was stillness, broken only by the gentle murmur of the current. The horrors of the headlines and television news reports seemed far away, and I was reminded that there are still some places on our earth where a divine plan for the universe seems to be unfolding as it should.

There have since been other fishing trips with my husband, my son, and more recently, my grandsons. We have shared something very special, and all because of one memorable day when I finally made peace with the river.

JEAN SCHNEIDER

NO ORDINARY YEAR

New Year's Eve started out as it always had in my family—celebrating the promise of a new year. At the stroke of midnight, I offered a toast to my husband. But suddenly, instead of the usual salute to my husband or to our family, I felt an urge to toast something completely different.

"This is going to be My Year," I proclaimed, surprising even myself at my self-centeredness. "I don't know why, I just feel like some great things are going to happen!" My husband looked at me, his expression doubtful. "I guess I'll drink to that," he replied.

How very prophetic my toast turned out to be! A month later, the day before my forty-third birthday, my husband moved out. He wanted some time to "find himself." I was devastated! He'd always had a tremendous amount of freedom within our marriage and in running his own company—his needing more was simply unimaginable to me.

I decided to file for a divorce and mend the loneliness that had crept into my life. The next few weeks were filled with anger, sadness, and more loneliness. Searching for clues as to how my marriage had so slowly and subtly deteriorated left me feeling perplexed and exhausted.

Soon after, at an out-of-town conference, I was alone in my hotel room. I decided it was time to quit feeling sorry for myself and to be myself again—optimistic and proactive. What if I just put together a list of all the characteristics that I would be looking for in a man? I had read about such an idea, and as far-fetched as it seemed, it couldn't hurt. At least I might be better able to recognize the right man if he did appear in my life. In preparing my list, I grouped the qualities I was seeking under the categories of physical, spiritual, professional, and educational. I ended up with twenty items in all. I was sure this particular man I'd created on paper would be my perfect complement. Putting the list in my day planner, I marveled at how long I'd been with a partner who no longer had the traits or interests that I desired in a life-long mate.

The very next day—although I didn't realize it at the time—I met a man who possessed each of the qualities I desired in a partner. On our first date, I became aware of the parallels in our lives and our shared sense of values. When I got home, I took another look at my wish list. This man seemed a very close match. The only item I wasn't sure of was whether he had blue eyes. That night, when we met for drinks, I caught his eye from across the room as he waved to me. There he sat with the warmest, kindest blue eyes I'd ever seen. How could this be? This kind of thing is something you hear about, not something that really happens. He'd appeared so suddenly that I wasn't sure I was ready just yet to meet my perfect mate!

As we became closer, I continued to marvel at our shared sense of playfulness and adventure. I knew I'd found my soul mate. One night I mentioned to him that I'd made a wish list in hopes of finding someone just like him. He laughed and said, "Well, if you've found someone this quickly, you must need a more specific list!" Of course, I had to show him the list after that comment. He looked it over, shaking his head in amazement.

As time progressed, our relationship continued to grow. Life seemed too perfect to believe—until I learned that because of a recent merger where I worked and overlapping responsibilities of similar positions in the two companies, I had not been selected to stay in my newly reorganized job. I looked out my office window and stared at the heart of downtown Denver. I didn't know whether to laugh or cry. My husband had deserted me and I'd filed for divorce, fallen in love, and lost my job, and it was only April. If this was the first four months of "my year," this was not going to be any ordinary year.

While I was lost in my thoughts, my secretary knocked at my door to tell me I had a visitor. I turned to see my new love coming toward me, offering me a bouquet of flowers. When I filled him in on the latest news, he said, "This new position would've taken so much of your energy. In many ways, I'm glad you didn't get it. Why don't you take some time and decide what you'd really love to do?"

I went home that night and took my boyfriend's advice to heart. I concluded it was time to trust my gut while I explored new job opportunities. My whole life was upside down compared to four short months ago. If there was ever a time to listen to my inner voice, this was it! So I did slow down, and I took the time I needed to find that next job.

The year has now passed. While, thankfully, not quite as fraught with the roller coaster of emotions of the first few months, it's been a wild one. My divorce was finalized, I've found new work that I love, and I married the wonderful man I met so quickly last year.

When I toasted "My Year," I had no idea what I might be in for. But I've learned a valuable lesson: no matter what's going on in my life, I can relax and watch it unfold as it will. What's more, from now on I'll pay attention when words fly out of my mouth during a toast. Sometimes our subconscious mind knows what's in store for us long before we do!

HOLLY FEDAK

VII
HOLIDAYS, HOPE,
AND HOLLY

Healthy families are our greatest natural resource.

DOLORES CURRAN

SAVOR THE SWEETNESS

*L*ogs crackle and golden flames leap and sparkle in the fireplace as Luther Vandross softly croons "Silent Night." Hundreds of miniature lights twinkle and glow, creating a dance of colors on the shiny red and silver packages stacked beneath the tree. We sip creamy, sweet eggnog sprinkled with just the right amount of nutmeg and inhale the earthy pine fragrance that fills the room. After an evening with friends and family, the two of us alone exchange our gifts, one by one—a Christmas Eve tradition born on our first Christmas together.

Memories of Christmases past float through my mind like a collage of old photographs . . . teenage newlyweds in our tiny apartment . . . our enchanting new angel with a white satin gown that adorned the top of a hopelessly crooked Christmas tree . . . our baby daughter's first Christmas, then our new son's . . . the fleeting, magical years as parents of young children . . . joyous, prosperous years as well as the three years that we struggled through unemployment but somehow managed to arrange visits from Santa.

Memories of two difficult Christmases wandered through my thoughts as well. After twenty years of marriage, we were financially secure and our children were almost grown. We had many dreams yet to fulfill. Sadly, we discovered that we had drifted apart. I didn't recognize the stranger who shared my home, nor he the silent, angry woman I'd become. We managed to hang on, to meet halfway on a bridge of compromises built on a strong foundation of love and respect, then found each other once again.

He smiles as he places the last gift in my hands, a box of Godiva, my favorite chocolates. I peel away the paper, lift the lid, and am surprised to find a letter neatly folded inside.

Dear Mimi,

We have shared twenty-eight Christmases together. The memories of some are so vivid that we will never forget them; our first Christmas as husband and wife, then as parents, special Christmases as a family, our "unemployed" Christmases. Some have been extraordinary and some have faded in our memories, but we know they, too, were special.

These chocolates represent those twenty-eight Christmases. They, like your memories, are yours to share or to keep for yourself. A few will be your favorites and the taste will linger. You will savor the sweetness long after the candy is gone. Some, although very good, will not be quite as delightful as others, but you will enjoy them and relish them nonetheless.

You will notice that two Godiva candies have been replaced with ordinary chocolate-covered walnuts. These symbolize the two years that we were both a little "nuts." Both pieces, like those two Christmases, are not quite as special as the rest, but remember, they are a part of the whole. Without them, there would not be twenty-eight. Also, you will notice that the box is not full. God willing, we will have many more Christmases to look forward to . . . and many, many more wonderful memories that we will cherish in the upcoming years.

I love you,

Joe

As I wrap my arms around him, my gaze falls upon our angel, smiling down from her place at the top of the tree. She's a little faded now, the hem of her satin skirt slightly tattered, but she, like our love, has endured and is radiant still.

MARGARET J. (MIMI) POPP

COURTING FAITH

It was in December when I made a decision to leave my husband. Early in the new year, I moved into my first apartment and began to learn about dating and life in the single world. Before I knew it, a year had passed.

That next Christmas, I bought a tiny tree and decorated it with handmade ornaments from my past. I stepped back to admire my handiwork, but instead walked around and around the little table I'd set the tree on, trying to figure out what was missing. Then I realized I'd never celebrated Christmas by myself; I'd always had someone special to share the holiday with. I dropped into a nearby chair, stared at the tree, and ached with loneliness. Just as I began to think about what the world might be like without me in it, a story my mother told me years before suddenly came to mind.

When Mom was a young woman she had wanted a baby boy so badly that she went to her church and put a note of her wish under a holy statue. Nine months later her firstborn son arrived.

I figured if it worked for Mom, it might work for me too. I wrote a letter to God and asked to meet someone who would love and respect me, someone who would treat me well and be faithful. I folded the letter and put it under my tiny tree.

One morning I lay in bed floating between dream and wake time. I saw a warm orange-pink color around the center of a bright light, felt a woman's gentle hand cradle my face as she told me without words, "Everything will be all right." I woke up, rolled over, and dialed Mom's number to tell her what had happened. "Maybe it was your guardian angel," she said in a sleepy voice.

A week later on a cold winter's night, I took a drive. A traffic light changed from green to yellow. I accelerated, trying to get through the intersection before the light turned red. As I sped through the light, I noticed a police car in my rearview mirror. I pulled over and waited for the officer to approach my car. I begged her not to give me a ticket, but she had to do her job. She handed me the ticket and wished me luck.

As I waited at traffic court for my name to be called, I noticed a handsome officer who worked in the courtroom. I watched him covertly, afraid he'd notice. When they called my name, I approached the judge's bench, pleaded no contest, and was directed to a desk on my right to sign some papers. The officer I'd found so attractive manned that desk.

"Hi, my name's Keith," he said. "You live in the same apartment complex as me." My stomach dropped, and I felt my face heat up.

"Stop in sometime," I heard myself offer, somewhat embarrassed.

"Sure." He grinned, squared my paperwork, and dropped it into a wire basket on the corner of his desk. Days passed, but I never saw him at the apartment.

Months later my girlfriend Torri called to get me out of the house for a trip to the mall. I tried to back out but she insisted. Not much in the mood for shopping, I kept my head down while we walked the mall and chatted. On our third lap Torri tugged me over to a kitchen display to check out the new gadgets. I didn't need any; I ate frozen dinners at home. At Torri's insistence, I looked up, and instead of a kitchen display, I saw my cute courtroom police officer watching me. Keith and I spoke for a few minutes, and he asked for my phone number. I tore a deposit slip out of the back of my checkbook and handed it to him.

Once he was out of earshot, I turned to Torri and said, "I'm the luckiest girl in the world!"

Christmas rolled around again. I went to the home of my stepbrother and his wife with my parents. I felt fortunate to enjoy the day with family, but as I waved and drove away, a blanket of depression slipped over me, and I asked, "God, why do I have to be alone?" An hour later, I pulled in at my apartment. Stillness and quiet covered the lot. I turned on the lights and flopped down on my bed. Out of the corner of my eye the message light on my answering machine blinked red. I rolled over and pushed PLAY. Keith's deep voice wished me a Merry Christmas!

Keith called again the day after Christmas, and we spoke for an hour and a half. The following day we had our first date in front of a fire with wine, music, and more talk. Since that date eight years ago, we haven't been apart a single day. Keith is that someone who loves and respects me, that someone who treats me well and is faithful in his love as my husband.

In His own time, God had answered my prayer in that folded letter under a tiny tree.

VALENTINA A. BLOOMFIELD

Christmas Eve was a night of song
that wrapped itself around you like a shawl.
But it warmed more than your body.
It warmed your heart.
BESS STREETER ALDRICH

STEEPED IN TRADITION

C hristmas Eve has always been the most special day of the year for me. I start in January, picking up stocking stuffers and gifts. I spend the entire year getting ready for this one night. Our children, spouses, and grandchildren—twenty-four in all—gather around the table for a night that each of us remembers. Gifts spill out of stockings and the table is covered with paper and ribbon, while singing and laughter abound. Christmas Eve dinner has become a family tradition.

When my children were small, I made a mistake and placed two of the same thing in a child's stocking. While the gifts were being opened, that child said to another across the table, "I'll trade you one of these for one of those." Each one flipped their exchange across the table, and that started the trading and tossing of gifts. Another family tradition was born.

My good friend Joan comes over a few days before Christmas Eve, and we spend the entire day wrapping gifts that have been hidden in the basement closet for a year. We start off wrapping each gift with care and creativity. By the end of the day, we're just tearing paper and twisting the ends together around the packages. Things look pretty bad, but we have a good time—singing and wrapping. Our husbands join us late in the afternoon, laugh at our mess, then the four of us have dinner together. This is tradition.

Every year, Joan wraps the baby Jesus and places him in the toe of someone's stocking. She never tells me how she decides who will have the honor of placing the baby in the manger to complete the nativity scene for the year. This is tradition.

But this year was different. We were without family or friends. Bud and I had taken a long, strenuous trip to Antarctica and returned just days before Christmas. Plus, we had recently moved to South Carolina from Illinois. We had decided before we left on our trip that it would be too much for us to unpack, repack, and board a plane for northern Illinois, where our children live. A bad decision!

Bud and I also figured that we wouldn't buy a gift for each other. Why just go out and buy something so that we each have a gift to open? Another bad decision!

While we were gone, I hired someone to come in and put up the Christmas tree and decorate it for us. I wanted to come home to Christmas. The tree was lovely, but it was Christmas without any spirit. This break from tradition pained me deeply.

When I count the years, I know that I'm old. In my way of thinking, the accumulation of years should equate to maturity. On this Christmas Eve, however, I spent the entire day feeling sorry for myself. Instead of a grandmother steeped in Christmas tradition, I felt like a two-year-old who wanted to hold on to her blanket and suck her thumb. I had nothing to do, and I missed my family. My children and their families celebrated in our daughter's home without us. This was not tradition.

Because of our trip, we had celebrated a mini-Christmas with some of our family at Thanksgiving. Only one lonely box, covered in brown UPS paper, appeared under our tree. How I missed those packages that Joan and I traditionally wrapped. How I missed the tossing of gifts and my laughing grandchildren.

About five o'clock on that blue Christmas Eve, my eyes filled with tears of remorse as our family gathered in another state to carry on our traditions built over the years. Bud suggested that we open the drab box from my daughter Julie and her husband. I went to the kitchen for a knife to cut the tape. I thought dejectedly, *Great, this should take all of a couple of minutes.* When I opened the box, I saw a tangled jumble of silver paper and string. I dumped the mess onto the table. Bud and I started to laugh. A good sign!

It took us about half an hour to untangle the string. We soon realized that "His" and "Hers" gifts were attached to the three-foot silver string. We started opening each one. His, a tube of Chapstick; Hers, a tube of lipstick. His, a charcoal lighter; Hers, a cigarette lighter. His, a flashlight; Hers, a spice apple candle that we immediately put on the table and lit. A wonderful fragrance immediately filled the air. "It's beginning to look a lot like Christmas," we both chimed at once. The gifts went on and on. By the time we'd finished opening the last one, we were laughing so hard that tears of joy were running down our cheeks.

Up until now, Bud and I had created the Christmas memories for our loved ones. This year, our daughter and her husband surprised us with their own unique ritual. Like the ceremonial passing of a baton already steeped in tradition, we can't wait to join our family next Christmas Eve to see what they have in store!

NANCY BUTLER

A CHRISTMAS TO
REMEMBER

Many years ago when our seven children were young, we began our family tradition of adopting a needy family for Christmas.

In the 1970s, when my husband and I took over the business from his dad, Rocker Electric Company consisted of one man and one woman. Henry did all the fieldwork, and I ran the office—or, rather, I should say the office ran me.

Most of our work was residential in those days, and sometimes I had to call customers and literally beg for some sort of payment. And so, as Christmas 1972 approached, I realized this was one of the worst financial years we'd ever experienced.

Even though I was able to purchase a few toys for each of our children, it was quite obvious there would be no new outfits this year. But most especially, how could we adopt a family—would we have to break our tradition?

One morning I noticed a full-page ad in our local paper. It said, "ONE DAY ONLY—WE'LL BUY YOUR SILVER AT PREMIUM PRICES! Bring your treasures to the Holiday Inn on I-10 Service Road in Metairie."

A bell went off in my head. We had never completed our silver service when we married, and it was packed away in a locker. I retrieved the box, and much to my amazement, I found five complete place settings of silver, miscellaneous serving pieces, and extra spoons and knives.

Henry and I smiled at each other and headed straight for the hotel. When the receptionist said "Take a number," I almost chickened out. I can still remember my feelings: disbelief that I was doing this, extreme embarrassment, and fear.

I recalled Matthew 7:7: "Ask, and it shall be given to you; seek and ye shall find; knock, and it shall be opened unto you." And so, as we sat there, I prayed, "Please, God, help us get enough money to adopt a family for Christmas. If we get just a hundred and seventy-five dollars, we can provide clothes, gifts, and food."

When our name was called, we went into the cubicle and presented our "treasure" to the appraiser. As he looked over each piece, I silently prayed, "Lord, please, at least a hundred and seventy-five dollars." The man finally spoke, "The best I can do for you is three hundred and twenty-five dollars." I almost fell out of the chair. Not only did we have enough money to adopt a family, our children could get new outfits and Christmas dinner would be a feast.

The old adage, "It is more blessed to give than to receive," proved true. This was, without a doubt, my most memorable Christmas.

RUTH ROCKER

It is possible to enjoy the music with companions
and to go deeper, to hear the oboe, alone.
JENNIFER JAMES

GIVING THANKS

*I*t has been four years since my husband, Marshall, died. He was my first love, and I was his. Our love grew through our twenty-five-year marriage, and a piece of my heart went with him.

At the funeral, our daughter, Rachel, bent over with grief, whispered to me, "Mom, I can't do this." I hugged her very close and replied, "Neither can I, so let's 'not do this' together."

That first year the pain was unrelenting, day and night. I was grateful for our Jewish rituals of mourning as they provided me with a structure to feel my grief. Sisterhood friends took over my kitchen after the funeral, surrounding me with caring and love. I soon joined a Jewish bereavement group. I could not say the word *widow* because then I would have to believe that Marshall had died. I listened and cried and wondered if the pain would ever be different, taking some comfort in knowing that we were all survivors.

My Thanksgiving this year was very different from so many before. In October, Rachel married Joshua in New York City. Both of them are busy, young attorneys creating a beautiful life together. Although Rachel had not lived at home for the past nine years, she'd always been able to fly home for the holiday. In the past, our small family of three often welcomed friends into our home for a joyful Thanksgiving feast. This year would represent a first—I would be alone for Thanksgiving.

Until now, I hadn't been paying attention to the real progress I was making on my healing journey. It surprised me, in fact, that I wasn't longing for a family of my own. I didn't feel like a child with my face pressed against a window, watching a happy family inside. I realized that I am my own family and I could choose to feel complete. So I spent time thinking about the many blessings in my life. I wanted to give voice to my thankfulness on this particular holiday.

I was grateful for the invitations I received from dear friends inviting me to their Thanksgiving dinner. But this year I wanted to shape and experience my own celebration.

So on Thanksgiving this year, I nourished myself. I felt safe and sheltered in my home once again. I bought deliciously prepared food, and I baked my own pumpkin pie. I built a fire and set the dining table with my best china and glassware. I lit candles and sat quietly, watching it grow dark outside while thinking of all the things I was grateful for. My three affectionate cats stayed close, purring loudly.

I played some of my favorite CDs and sipped sparkling cider. I said blessings out loud, thanking friends who regularly write and call from faraway places, those I talk with daily, and the ones I see often. I sent loving wishes to Joshua and Rachel and to Rachel's new extended family. I blessed all whom I love, and I stroked my cats.

I remembered past Thanksgivings in different places—with dear friends in their vacation home alongside a beautiful river where candlelight reflected smiling faces inside, and the snow was falling outdoors—with the family who welcomed me into their circle when I was working in New York, thousands of miles from home—and of course, with Marshall and Rachel for all our

Thanksgivings together. I found myself thinking that from now on I'll build new traditions that will, in turn, become more happy memories.

On this Thanksgiving, I ate slowly, savoring the different tastes and textures on my plate. My daily morning walk on a nearby track had been in stormy weather. Soaked to the skin, I laughed aloud at my dripping hair, my wet clothes, and the puddles in my shoes. I exchanged greetings with a few other faithful walkers. Two large dogs jumped up to lick my face. On the way home, I sang "Singing in the Rain." It turned out to be a magical Thanksgiving. Marshall always wanted me to be happy, and at last, I do believe I am.

Not long after, I had my wedding ring made into a small gold heart, which I hung on a chain. My women's group surrounded me and fastened this necklace around my neck. It was then that I could finally say, "I am a widow." I live by myself, yet I do not feel alone.

CAROLE R. ROTSTEIN

A TIME FOR ALL SEASONS

Charlie Brown's Christmas *theme music bounces* around the room. I deck the fresh and fragrant tree with the funny-faced reindeer made of clothespins and felt scraps, the painted clay bells from Mexico, the scratched plastic ornaments, still whole and still hung on the Christmas tree since baby's first Christmas. Seven snow-white doves sewn of cotton cloth by poor women in El Salvador contrast against the deep green of the boughs. It is the first Sunday of Advent, and this is our Advent ritual: to bring home the tree, to struggle it into an upright position in the red metal stand, and to adorn it with talismans of Christmases past.

We had our first Christmas together in our tiny studio apartment across the street from the university. It was very romantic—just the two of us, our eyes and hopes brighter than any of the colored lights on our own Christmas tree.

Christmas in our first house was the year that the tree was a small one mounted on a large cardboard box wrapped in red paper and broad white ribbon to resemble a gift. This was to protect it from the curiosity of our firstborn, who at the age of ten months was pulling herself up, exploring from a new perspective.

By the following year we had two babies, one still in a bassinet, the other old enough and wise enough to pull the tree down on top of herself. Enter the plastic ornaments suitable for wee ones. A third daughter joined the clan, and by our eighth Christmas she was a year and a half old. She had never tasted candy until that Christmas, when she had a stocking full. My favorite photo shows her standing in the new bright yellow surrey with the red fringed top, her baby blue blanket sleeper sticky with pink candy cane drool, the cane clutched firmly in her right fist.

Two more years passed, and the family was growing too large for the little ranch house. By the following Christmas we were in a big old two-story with a grand mantelpiece for hanging Christmas stockings. A month after that first Christmas in our new home, baby number four arrived. The next year the gifts under the tree included a Notre Dame football helmet from the baby's uncle. This was a contrast to the girls' gifts: the game of Clue, Liddle Kiddles, and the plastic baby doll, who, within a year, would be tattooed with purple Magic Marker and have a grid of grimy tufts on her head where hair once "grew."

Each December now, the children made a crèche. A cardboard carton was cut to make a stable; the figures were made from Play-Doh. The oldest child made the Blessed Virgin, which required a certain level of skill to distinguish her as the only female in the scene. Joseph, the baby Jesus, the shepherds, the three kings, and the donkey and cow were less challenging. The youngest child always got to make the Wise Men's camels. Almost any shape could represent a camel. The older children gave the camel creator a bit of each color to smash together until a brownish shade was achieved. The resulting lump could be a camel standing, a camel lying down, a camel stretching, or perhaps a camel snapping at a fly that had landed on its rump.

When baby boy was three, a baby sister completed the family. From then on, the tree was surrounded by a mound of wrapped packages from cousins, from Mom and Dad, from each other, and on Christmas morning from Santa. Soon the entire living room floor was a sea of gift wrap.

Each year the number of toys shrank and the number of clothes increased, until at last the grown children were fewer in number as each began to set up her or his own Christmas tree in a new home.

This year we set up our tree and decorated it right after Thanksgiving—just the two of us. The gifts under the tree will come from our faraway children and from each other. We will sit in front of the fireplace and drink eggnog and see the warm glow of love in each other's eyes. It will be so romantic!

ALBERTA JAMES DAW

VIII
TOUGH ON ISSUES, SOFT ON PEOPLE

One is not born a woman, one becomes one.

SIMONE DE BEAUVOIR

THE TERRIBLE WHYS

When our son Kyle was born, my husband and I worried about living far from our parents. The baby's arrival seemed to triple the distance between Texas and Pennsylvania. We knew we would never enjoy the convenience of grandparents, as our parents had when we were children. The telephone was really no substitute for a trip to Grandma's house. As a result, I turned to books, magazines, and friends for advice.

Although I would never admit it to my husband, I also worried about having a boy. After all, I knew girls better. Most of my friends had girls. I'd spent years dreaming of velvet Christmas dresses, black patent leather shoes, ballet lessons, nail polish, and canopy beds. As I had progressed through my pregnancy, and discovered we'd have a boy, I quietly packed my frilly fantasies and resolved to do my best to understand the male point of view. After Kyle arrived, new motherhood kept me too occupied to think about whether I'd be happier with a girl.

The first two years passed without incident, except that Kyle walked at seven months. That meant baby-proofing the house earlier than we had expected. Even the dreaded "terrible twos" weren't so bad once I'd mastered the art of offering choices. Many days I felt I'd made more deals than Monty Hall. But for the most part, I survived the second year with my sanity intact.

However, the third year caught me completely unprepared. All the parenting magazines seemed to jump from the terrible twos into something called "the preschool years," skipping the third year and leaving me to rely on experience. The threes, I learned, were a particularly trying time, especially for parents. And, it seemed to me, especially for parents of boys.

If the anthem for two-year-olds is "No," the three-year-old's battle cry is "Why." A three-year-old's entire existence consists of discovery. At first, I enjoyed helping Kyle learn about the world. Very quickly, though, I surmised that any conversation with him could reduce even the most logical person to a completely heartless idiot. Kyle frequently substituted "What's that" for "Why," turning trips to the grocery store into instant quiz shows. Although I appreciated Kyle's curiosity, I struggled to answer all the questions. I hated myself when I allowed exasperation to overwhelm me and finally replied, "Because that's the way it is, Kyle."

Why's counterpart was "carpe diem." Every fiber of Kyle's being was dedicated to exploration and celebration, through questions, movement, and language. For months I believed the child couldn't walk normally; he ran, danced, hopped, or jumped every time he moved. Longingly, I watched little girls at church who sat quietly looking at picture books or playing with dolls while Kyle triple-somersaulted off the pew. Before long, Kyle began experimenting with language. He seldom spoke without shouting, singing, or imitating the animal du jour. A simple task, like getting into the car, often took ten minutes by the time I answered all the whys, explored every rock in the driveway, and attempted to strap a dancing child into a car seat.

I envied Kyle's passion. But my practical nature, ever driven by schedules, deadlines, meetings, and appointments, became increasingly frustrated. Moreover, the phone calls home for advice only increased my isolation. My mother, who had raised both boys and girls, pointed out to me that Kyle was a normal, albeit overly curious, little boy. Brian's mother, who'd had more experience with boys, didn't think anything was out of the ordinary either. "If you lived closer," both grandmas reiterated, "you could drop him with me for the weekend. Then you'd have a new perspective."

Help arrived when I least expected it. One summer day, Kyle and I hurried to a routine doctor's appointment. As usual, Kyle had occupied himself with the busy task of discovery while I hurried us through the parking garage in an attempt to arrive promptly. In desperation, I bent to pick him up when the elevator doors suddenly opened. Kyle executed a perfect standing broad jump, and was met by delighted applause.

"What a perfect leap you made," cried a grandmotherly woman. Kyle beamed. "Would you like to push the buttons?" she asked.

Proudly, Kyle's chubby hands jammed all the elevator buttons at once as he smiled at his new friend.

"I had five boys," she said. "They've all grown up and moved away now. But I still remember what times we had when they were young."

The elevator stopped at every floor, and I found myself laughing along with Kyle and our mentor. Suddenly arriving on time did not seem so very important. With the help of a stranger, I began to appreciate the "terrible whys" and little boys.

LAURIE HOPKINS ETZEL

THE INVISIBLE WOMAN

As I stroll past my neighborhood construction site, I notice how men's heads turn when they take me in from top to bottom. Then it happens, almost overnight. Just days later, right after my fortieth birthday, the same heads look up in weakened recognition, then eagerly resume munching their overstuffed heros.

I never deliberately sought this attention. It's just that it had been there for a very long time. I had become accustomed to it like background muzak in the mall. It began in my teens, when the cumbersome braces came off and my small-boned figure blossomed with a few womanly curves, probably from those chocolate malteds my mother insisted I drink lest I slip through the cracks in the sidewalk on the way to school.

Now, I take this first season of no notice in good stride. After all, it is still winter. Who can really see me covered from head to toe with only a few wisps of blond hair peeking out of my beret? But then spring arrives. There are girl watchers everywhere: businessmen out for a stroll, tempted by fresh warm breezes; and rows of muscular hard hatters lining the marble steps of office buildings.

I used to prepare myself for walking past these hordes of men, promising not to make any direct eye contact. And I will admit that, as long as I didn't hear any lewd reference to a particular body part or sexual act, I actually enjoyed the soft mumblings of admiration. It all seemed so harmless. Their gawking never made me feel spiritually or emotionally raped. Most of the time, I found it amusing.

But now I am suddenly aware that there are few admirers for my new figure-flattering pantsuit. At first I blame it on a bad haircut, but as summer approaches and my sun-streaked tresses reach shoulder length, there are still no rave reviews from my street fans. So, I opt for a lunchtime peel, invest in a free radical combative moisturizer, and adopt the "less is more" approach to cosmetic application.

I rationalize that I'd been slacking off at the gym; maybe I need a little tune-up. It's time to add some cross training to my workout and free weights to keep the bones honed. By midsummer I am determined to test-drive an improved, svelte me.

I position myself at all the prime locations, knowing where the boys are: trade shows and sporting events. But all I hear one night, at a major league ball game, is a polite " 'scuse me, ma'am" as a couple of burly guys step over my pedicured toes on the way back to their seats. I'd been called ma'am before, but never by somebody my own age.

Frustrated but still hopeful, I go home and peer into my mirror. For the most part I like what I see. I'm not entirely washed up just because some of my angles have taken a sharp turn and headed south. I call some close friends and ask them to be honest: Have I really fallen apart? Am I delusional to think I still look really good? One friend tells me to be grateful I don't live in L.A.

"There you'd be invisible before thirty," she huffs. "You've had an extra decade!"

She's right, but I still can't shake that nagging feeling of having misplaced something. And why do I allow myself to put so much value in the judgment of others, not to mention complete strangers?

On a long walk during lunch hour, I become sort of a hidden camera. I try focusing on what the rest of the world is viewing. But there is no huge mystery to unfold here, no great revelation for my brain to tabulate. Somewhere, in my all-too-youthful heart, I've known the truth all along.

Most people, especially in this U. S. of A., turn hastily from the aging to revere the young. Don't they know that Twiggy, Christy, and even Barbie have passed forty? But no matter how well preserved you are at forty or fifty . . . you simply aren't twenty. And who exactly have I been gaping at all these fleeing years with admiration, disguising envy? I still read magazines whose covers represent the promise of youthfulness and beauty—whose demographics are years younger than myself. I, too, have placed the idea of an eternal spring at the forefront.

Some enlightenment comes as my mental hidden camera focuses on an elegant, gray-haired gentleman. Perhaps he's nearing sixty. He is smiling at me when my eyes quickly pan away from him and do a freeze-frame on two twenty-something hunks striding down the street, dressed in pinstripes—donning shades. I zoom back to the gentleman, taking him in warmly, completely. Suddenly, for me, he is a most welcome minority in a throng of younger faces.

SANDE BORITZ BERGER

It kills you to see them grow up.
But I guess it would kill you quicker if they didn't.
BARBARA KINGSOLVER

MY DAUGHTER,
THE RAGGED INDIVIDUALIST

When my daughter, Elizabeth, began preschool, no one prepared us for the damaging effects of peer pressure—on her mother.

It started the very first week. Although the teacher had recommended dressing the kids in play clothes, the three-year-olds in Elizabeth's class looked as if they were on a photo shoot for *Preschooler's Bazaar*. The Other Moms of girls, especially, had dressed their daughters to impress in darling, "aah"-inspiring pants outfits and matching hair bows.

Bows? Forget it—my free-spirited daughter barely let me brush her hair. But pants we could do. Elizabeth *liked* pants. I dashed out to our local mall. One empty wallet and a full closet later, Elizabeth had a selection of cute pants and tops I was sure all the Other Moms would love.

The next school day, Elizabeth announced, "I *hate* pants. I want to wear dresses. *Just* dresses."

Using an argument I knew I would want to reject ten years later, I said, "But none of the other girls wear dresses."

"I don't care," she said. "I want to wear this." She pulled out of the closet her official party dress, a flouncy, ruffles-and-lace number her grandmother had bought for her.

"How about this?" I countered, pointing to a plainer dress—one she wears to church on Sunday.

"No!" she said. "It has long sleeves. I hate long sleeves." Since when? Rampaging through her closet again, Elizabeth struggled into a faded Notre Dame T-shirt and a pleated, white polyester skirt I had picked up at a yard sale. "This is what I'll wear," she announced. With her hands defiantly on her hips, Elizabeth looked like a tiny cheerleader whose team has just gotten a bad call from the ref.

She also looked clean and comfortable. So I gave in—"Just this time." But, deaf to pleas or flattery ("Ooh, let me see how pretty you would look in these pink pants"), Elizabeth wore either the white skirt or its bright blue twin (bought at the same yard sale) and a short-sleeved T-shirt for each and every one of her preschool classes that fall. Luckily—or unluckily, I wasn't sure—what my husband began to call "Elizabeth's uniform" remained unfrayed despite many washings.

My ego was unraveling, though. I fretted that the Other Moms would think I didn't have the taste, the money, or, worse yet, the love to dress my little girl well. By following her own strict dress code, Elizabeth was making *me* look bad.

As the weather got colder, Elizabeth switched from anklets to tights (sometimes wearing both). That was the only substitution permitted; she wore short-sleeved tees well into December. One subfreezing day, I stepped over a pile of rejected clothes and—I'm ashamed to admit—some sort of mental line, too. "What's so bad about long sleeves?" I shouted. Elizabeth said, tears in her eyes, "What's so important about long sleeves?"

What is so important? I scolded myself. Elizabeth didn't need long sleeves for warmth—Lord knows her bulky coat, mittens, and hat would protect her for the three-minute walk from parking lot to school. I could leave a sweater with the teachers for her to put on if the playroom got chilly. When you think about the paints, glue, and glitter that preschoolers get their hands into, short sleeves probably are better. And, as far as I knew, none of the other kids had told Elizabeth that her ensembles lacked imagination. (True, none of the Other Moms had ever complimented me on her clothes, either.)

Despite visions of those darling pant sets fading, unwanted and unheralded, in Elizabeth's closet, I ended the wardrobe war then and there. Ever since, I have—calmly, if morosely—let Elizabeth choose her own outfits. The white (or blue) skirt remains her favorite. I've trained myself to look past its faded spots to focus on my daughter's shining face. So I smile when one of the Other Moms says, "She really loves that skirt, doesn't she?" and I chuckle when another teases, "Here comes your cheerleader." I laughed loudest, though, the other day when a mom said, sighing, "Katie tells me she wants to wear only skirts, just like Elizabeth."

My daughter, that ragged individualist, has won the respect of her peers—and my respect, too. No doubt our closet skirmishes were just the first of many declarations of independence Elizabeth and I will have to work through. Just wait until the teen years, my older friends warn. For now, one of those more experienced moms has come up with a practical way to disentangle my ego from Elizabeth's fashion choices—a campaign-button-size pin that says "Not dressed by her mother" or, even better, "I dressed myself."

That might work—*if* I can convince Elizabeth to wear it.

Elizabeth McGinley

FINDING THE
MUSIC

Would this be it?

Thoughts of never playing guitar again drew me to tears as I walked into the band room for the last time. I was a little bit nervous, but I could see no other way to get my half stack, all my effect pedals, and my guitar back without confronting the other members. Two thousand dollars' worth of equipment simply could not be left behind.

So much had happened in this room. We took songs and turned them into masterpieces for Florida's only all-female rock band, Black Widow. We had played all over the state, won Battle of the Bands, and even had famous people stopping by our practices and inviting us to be their opening acts. And, through it all, Dawn, Kristen, Michele, and I became the best of friends.

Walking in, I took one last look at where so many incredible times had passed. The drum set sat in the corner, the sticks lay on the snare drum, Kristen's bass guitar and amplifier stood in the far corner next to my half stack, and in the center of the room stood Michele's red lipstick–smeared microphone stand. I wiped my tear-stained face, and I thought I would be sick as I loaded my guitar case into my car.

A large piece of me felt like it was dying.

I called the lead singer, Michele, later that day and told her I had to quit the band. I told her I was pregnant, and my husband

and I thought it would be best since all those road trips would be hard on a baby.

It hurt so badly to hang up that phone. Michele didn't say a word, but I knew she was as crushed as I was.

Not only would I never be a famous guitarist, but I broke up the sound and crushed Black Widow's dreams too. I threw my guitar case in the corner and did not touch it.

Life went on. I nursed my mother through terminal cancer and raised two beautiful babies into young girls. I learned embroidery, painting, and some treasured motherly things.

Instead of writing songs, I started writing poetry and even became internationally published. I did aerobics every day, and Michele, to my surprise, stayed my closest friend.

Still, no matter how hard I tried to forget, I would dream about playing in the band. I could still feel the smooth guitar neck in my hand as my fingers danced gracefully over the strings. I could feel the beat of the drums pounding in my chest, hear Michele's beautiful, strong voice and the roar of the crowd when we finished a song.

On New Year's Eve, I couldn't stand it any longer. It was a rare occasion; I was up late and had taken a drink. I pulled the guitar out of the case and somehow found the courage to run my hand over the badly oxidized strings.

The children were sound asleep, so I started to play my Ibenez quietly in a darkened room. The notes rung in my ear like whispers from heaven.

I had forgotten the songs, but I created a new tune off the top of my head, strumming it until my fingers blistered.

That night, I cried myself to sleep, but this time the tears weren't from sadness but from joy, because I'd finally remembered what brought me the pleasure of being in a band. It wasn't the fame. It wasn't the money. It was the music flowing from my heart straight into my fingers.

Now I play guitar and sing with a new awareness of my love of music. I play and sing lullabies to my children at bedtime, and I play and sing love songs to my husband. And I play and sing for myself. My soul has found its voice once again.

DAWN KREISELMAN

LESSONS FROM THE WATER FOUNTAIN

I stood at the edge of the playground and signaled for the children to gather. Some thirty sweaty and soiled kindergartners ran, or sauntered, to line up at a nearby drinking fountain, as was our daily routine. I stood at the fountain turning the water on and off. "One, two, three—next," I slowly said as they took their turns and filed down the corridor to an awaiting teacher in our classroom. Suddenly, running from across the schoolyard came Corbin. He slid into a place close to the front of the line and hoped to go unnoticed. However, his feet were barely planted when a chorus of whining began: "Corbin butted. Corbin didn't go to the end of the line. Move, Corbin. Teacher, Corbin . . ."

I interrupted the singsong. "Corbin, are you forgetting to take your proper place?" This was my attempt to allow our young student to rebound with dignity. Corbin looked stubbornly ahead. "Corbin, please go to the end of the line." I raised my voice and became more authoritative. Corbin's lower lip pushed forward, and he studied his Batman shoelaces, but didn't move a muscle or his firmly planted feet. "Well, it looks like I need to help you," I suggested, and relinquished my on-off faucet job to Jennifer, gently reached for Corbin's hand, and led him to the back of the line. As I turned to leave, Corbin yelled, "I hate you, Ms. Resh!"

Calmly, I turned, bent down, looked directly at Corbin, and said, "Wow, I can tell you are really angry. We need to talk about this privately at nap time. Until then, I want you to know I still like you, and I don't like being shouted at that way. Now I need to see that everyone gets a drink." Then I returned to the faucet to resume my task. "Thank you, Jennifer, for being a nice helper." I smiled and continued, "One—two—three—next," at a little faster pace. When our line caboose, Corbin, took his drink, I noticed his glare but chose to ignore it. The two of us walked without a word back to our room, where we continued our morning routine.

We washed up, read a story, listened to "The Yawning Song," and finally settled down, somewhat reluctantly, for nap time. I put on my furry pink slippers and helped the children place various-colored mats in their familiar spots. When at last it was quiet, I approached Corbin and motioned with my finger for him to come with me. The curious onlookers knew it was our time to find a better way to deal with life's little problems.

I opened the door to the outside, and Corbin followed close behind. We sat cross-legged on the grassy ground for our pow-wow. I leaned forward and looked directly into the big, brown eyes of this five-year-old and said, "Corbin, what do you hate about me?" I waited patiently for a reply as Corbin lowered his head and studied his fidgety fingers. No response. "Did someone or something upset you before school or on the playground this morning?" Again I waited. Again no response. I drew in a long breath and said, "Well—maybe I can help you figure this out. Perhaps you were just mad because I didn't allow you to have your way. You wanted to be one of the first to get your drink, when you were the very last one to line up. Am I right?" His eyes never looked up. No response. "Perhaps you forgot I'm here to help everyone in this room get along. Sometimes you are first and sometimes you are last. We are all friends, and friends take turns. This helps make our classroom a safe and fun place to be. Do you understand?" Corbin lifted his curly brown head slightly and nodded up and down. "Is there anything you want to tell me?" No verbal response; however, I clearly understood his body language as he shook his head from side to side. "Okay, then, you get back on your mat and take a rest, and I'll bet you'll feel much better when you get up."

As I closed the door to the outside, I questioned my method of handling the situation. I doubted our powwow had left a meaningful impression on Corbin, let alone settled any of life's little problems. I convinced myself to let it go and move on. I had done my best.

Back in the room, I watched Corbin return to his blue mat, then I took my fuzzy pink slippers on our customary mat rounds, stooping occasionally to rub the small back of a restless child or to whisper "Shhh." Finally, I sat down in the nearly dark room to review our afternoon activities. As I concentrated on my paperwork in the much-appreciated silence, I felt a soft tap on my shoulder. I lifted my eyes, turned slowly, and there stood Corbin. His tan face revealed a very sheepish grin. Before I could collect my thoughts, he blurted out, "Ms. Resh, I don't hate you anymore. I want to be your friend." My blue eyes met his big brown ones, and as he threw his arms around my neck, we squeezed each other tightly. No words were really needed, yet I managed to say, "Thank you, Corbin."

I still wonder if he saw the tear that trickled down my cheek or heard my heart sing. If so, he didn't say a word. He just slowly turned around, and I watched his small stockinged feet tiptoe and weave very carefully around his sleeping friends as he made his way back to his blue mat that was stationed in its familiar spot—in the middle of thirty adorable kindergartners.

LINDA RESH

There are no shortcuts to any place worth going.
BEVERLY SILLS

ONE MORE MILE

he early-morning sun had barely peeked over the hills when I heard Catharina's upbeat Swedish chanting, "One more mile, ya? So much fun, ya?"

I glanced behind me at our blond, energetic boot camp director, disgust etched on my face. Catharina, known to the recruits as "the laughing saint," insisted that all of us future fitness buffs could hike up the steep fire trail.

I had signed up for the two-week endurance program at the Ashram Retreat to get healthy. Years as a struggling actress in Hollywood and being bulimic to keep my weight down had physically and emotionally taken their toll. I was living in the dark dank at the bottom and the retreat was my last hope. When I read the brochure, I actually believed it would be fun . . . like a spa.

I soon learned a normal day at the ashram meant up and out of bed before dawn. Breakfast was juice, followed by yoga with stretches, a five-mile hike . . . usually straight up the mountain, and weight-lifting class. A soak in the pool to soothe my aching muscles turned into water exercises and playing volleyball. Lunch was usually a fresh salad, celery, carrot sticks, and all the water we could drink. Then came nap time. I actually convinced myself it was a ploy to keep us alive. The rest of the day consisted of two miles around the track, another challenging hike, exercise class, and more stretching in the meditation dome.

Everyone complained bitterly the first day. The second day, everyone complained. Our main goal was how to get through each day. A camaraderie of support began to build among the women. "C'mon, you can do it," was echoed during the endurance hikes and on the running track. We received eight pebbles prior to running. After each full turn, we would drop a pebble until all were gone, and we could quit. I wanted to cheat and drop two pebbles at a time, but Catharina's sharp eyes missed nothing. She would laugh off our complaints and quip, "You are all so cute. Dis is really fun, ya? One more mile."

I remember well the day we sat down for lunch in sweats, T-shirts, and stringy hair, and a new guest was introduced. A reporter from *Vogue* magazine. We all just stared at her in awe. She was cosmetic counter perfection, not a hair out of place. I wolfed down my juice, a tuna-stuffed papaya, and even ate the papaya skin. All the while "Miss Vogue" was watching me . . . appalled. Two days later, I didn't blink an eye when I saw her again, disheveled like the rest of us, eating her papaya skin. That was the beauty of the ashram. It diminished the judgment side in all of us. I discovered that the more miles I hiked, the less I concentrated on the physical pain and the more I focused on my inner strength and values. I realized, each day, Catharina was pushing me one more mile closer to my intrinsic self.

When I left the ashram two weeks later, I was healthy, pounds lighter, my skin glowed, and my energy was at an all-time high. Then something happened to trigger a return visit. The night before I turned thirty, I went out to dinner with my boyfriend. I looked forward to a beautiful celebration of champagne, a gourmet dinner, and my favorite chocolate cream cake. We were sitting in the finest restaurant in Beverly Hills. He smiled from across the table and handed me a small velvet box. Inside was a lovely piece of jewelry.

"Happy Birthday. I'm glad you like it," he said. "And by the way, I'm really sorry, but I went back to my old girlfriend . . . Honey, why aren't you finishing your meal?"

I was devastated. As soon as I got home that night, I called Catharina. "My thirtieth birthday is tomorrow," I wailed, "and my boyfriend just dumped me for another woman."

"That's no good," she replied. "You be here tomorrow morning at six sharp, ya? I'll be waiting."

I celebrated my thirtieth . . . hiking twelve miles, drinking plain water, and munching all the fresh fruit and veggies I could eat. My party outfit was sweats and sneakers. That night I sat surrounded by candles in the meditation dome, gazing at the stars.

I had written my script one way, but, surprisingly, it had played out a better way. I thought the ashram would make me beautiful, so I could attract the man and the life I wanted. But I realized I was living a more honest life in my grungy sweats, eating papaya. The friendship and support of the other women taught me it didn't matter what you did but who you were. Acceptance and courage are not something we wear on the outside of our skin.

The ashram experience put me in touch with the unique me. Not the one I had tried to become, or who I was in a love affair, or the person I was yesterday. I was becoming as I was meant to be. My gift on my thirtieth birthday was simple and profound. I discovered that when you make yourself healthy on the inside, you will be equipped to go another one of life's extra miles.

DONNA HARTLEY

I LEARNED IT ON THE FARM

Grandma and Grandpa lived in a house on five hundred acres, and I was lucky enough to live across the road. They owned a little general store in a hamlet called Cloyne, in Ontario, Canada. Grams was known locally for her homemade chocolate and vanilla ice cream. Whenever I had playmates over, they would always get me to ask Grams for ice cream cones. She never disappointed me by saying no.

Gramps worked hard, went to church, and loved his garden, telling stories and eating a nightly bedtime snack of toast with maple syrup and ice cream.

When I turned sixteen, I immediately got my driver's license, and the first thing I did was take Gramps to Kingston to buy him an ice cream cone at the place with thirty flavors. Gramps didn't waste any time contemplating the display case; he walked right up and ordered vanilla.

I couldn't believe it. I'd driven sixty-five miles into town and he ordered vanilla! I tried not to show my disappointment, but Gramps must have picked up on it, because he said, "Life's like ice cream. In the old days, you had a choice, chocolate or vanilla. But today you've got soooo many choices. Look at this place." Gramps swept his weathered palm from one end of the display to the other. "Thirty kinds of ice cream makes it tough to choose. There's nothing wrong with vanilla. It's simple, good, and I enjoy it." Gramps took a bite of his cone, and I ran my tongue around the ice cream in mine. "Simplicity has its advantages," Gramps continued. "Technology's made everything so complicated. Not that cars and phones aren't handy, but too much technology gives you too many choices, which isn't always good. Too many ways to turn can bring you to a dead stop in the middle of the road, and while you're standing there scratching your head trying to figure out which way to go, life keeps moving right on by."

Years later, I came face-to-face with one of those stop-in-the-middle-of-the-road choices. I was unmarried and unexpectedly expecting my first child. There were soooo many choices. Abortion, adoption, adoption planned in advance with a chosen adoptive couple, raising the child on my own. Gramps said, "Let's face it, lots of folks are single parents. Make the decision that's best for you and the child. Folks'll talk, but news today is lost tomorrow."

My grandparents have since passed on, but first they saw me embrace my son into my life, then marry and have a second child. Their wisdom and insight are still with me as I guide my children through life. Like Grams and Gramps, I will be supportive, kind, and loving to my children and others. To keep me in touch with my roots, I will tell my kids the things that Grams and Gramps said to me. Like, "To be genuine, you need to look people in the eye. A smile and a thank-you will take you a long way. And whatever situation you're in, just be sincere and keep it simple. Things always work out for the best."

As Grams and Gramps' legacy is passed on, my children will know that fewer choices does not mean less opportunity—it could also mean a better way of life.

Whenever I get caught up in the hectic pace of working full-time, running kids back and forth, trying to be a good housekeeper, wife, friend, and superwoman, I make myself stop and reflect on what I'm doing. When I have time, I pack up the car and head for the family farm where Grams and Gramps once lived. If time is scarce, I close my eyes and imagine I'm there, the warmth of my morning mug of coffee between my hands as I sit on the porch of the log cabin watching the sun rise. I hear my breathing slow to an even cadence in the country silence, and feel the presence of the blessed simplicity I always found with Grams and Gramps.

DEBORAH MILLS-ELDER

IX
KEEPING THE
MEMORIES ALIVE

Sow good services;
sweet remembrances will grow from them.

MME. DE STAËL

A FATHER'S LENS

I was eleven years old before my father finally acknowledged my constant requests and allowed me to use his prized Canon AE-1 camera. I will never forget that first thrill of a real camera in my hands. Hardly believing my luck, I snapped away, sneaking up stealthily on my subject matter, the elusive white-tailed deer. I promptly shot two entire rolls of deer-in-the-underbrush. When seventy-two exposures of nondescript grass and shrubs came back seemingly devoid of subject matter, I was, to say the least, disappointed.

My father was annoyed. I'd wasted vacation film—a cardinal sin. I pointed out the microscopic specks in the photos defensively: "See, Dad, they're deer, just look!" He seemed less than impressed. It was a while before he let me use his camera again.

My next quarry was a hummingbird. It whirred into our backyard for a fraction of a second one summer afternoon and hovered near a clump of scarlet flowers. I was so sure that my father would want photographic documentation of this miraculous event that I "borrowed" his camera without actually asking permission. I waited and waited for the bird to return, but to no avail. I waited so long, in fact, that I forgot my quest totally and went inside. I left the camera outside. Overnight. And, as luck would have it, it rained. When I realized what I'd done, I was mortified, and certain I would be grounded until I was at least twenty. I knew I'd totally blown it. Fortunately, the camera was not permanently damaged, but it would rightfully be a really long time until I had Dad's camera in my hands again.

It didn't happen until I was sixteen, in fact. I had just won a trip to England in an essay/interview contest. I couldn't believe that I was actually going to Europe. What I couldn't believe even more was that Dad asked me if I'd like to take his camera with me. This being the trip of a lifetime, he thought I might want to get some good pictures of it.

I was fairly dumbstruck. "You really mean it?" I asked in awe. Looking back, I think the camera was his own kind of Dad safety charm. It was an extension of him, a symbolic form of protection to ensure that I came home in one piece.

At sixteen, I didn't know what it meant to be a parent. I didn't know how difficult it was to worry, to set misgivings aside, to smile, and then to let go. I was young enough to actually think that it was harder for him to let me take his camera on my trip than it was for him to let me travel abroad by myself.

The day I graduated from high school Dad pulled me into the kitchen. "Karen," he said, "your graduation present is on the table in the hall." He looked excited. "I hope you like it." The only thing on the table was his camera. He walked into the hall and stood behind me. He put his hands on my shoulders. "I'd like for you to have my camera," he said by way of explanation. For once in my teenage life, I was totally at a loss for words. "I was going to buy you a new one, a better one, but I knew how much you liked mine, and I thought this one would mean more to you. I thought a new one might not be the same." And he was right. Dad had given me more than a just a camera, even more than a cherished belonging of his own. He had just given me the evidence of his trust, his benediction. My father had given me a modern-day rite of passage. No gift he could have given me, no matter how new or how expensive, would have meant more.

That was half my lifetime ago.

Since that day, Dad's camera has been with me on tops of mountains and volcanoes, in alpine meadows, at sunrises and sunsets. It's been to family reunions, graduations, weddings, holiday gatherings, and delivery rooms. It's seen my first car and my first boyfriend, who later became my first (and only) husband. It saw my first bad perm and my first gray hair. It saw our first new home, our first out-of-state move. It saw my first-, second-, and third-born children on their first day of life. Now it regularly records their firsts.

With so much new camera technology lately, sometimes I'm fleetingly tempted to buy something flashier to replace Dad's Canon. But whenever I see the well-worn black leather case, I think of my father and his gift. I think of him when I press down the shutter button and hear the familiar click as the film advances on my life. I think of my father's blessing to me and how it has become part of his legacy. A father's lens on a daughter's life. And then I know one thing. Something my father himself taught me. Newer might possibly be better, but it could never be the same.

KAREN C. DRISCOLL

When you cease to make a contribution, you begin to die.
ELEANOR ROOSEVELT

MAKING A DIFFERENCE

O ur thirty-fifth James F. Byrnes High School reunion in Duncan, South Carolina, waxed wild and
wonderful for a few of us fifty-pluses. A live band
played stomping good oldies like "That Old-Time Rock 'n Roll."
Sad thing was, too many vegetated in their seats and merely ob-
served, marking time till dinner passed, yawning, then, with considerable relief, departing.

My husband, Lee, and I were fellow graduates, and we helped
host the evening. I mentally tallied absentees who'd not shown
their faces since high school graduation. And while many lived
distances away, an alarming number were locals who could have
come. Lordy, if only we could bond! Then we could make a difference in each other's lives. *But how?* I wondered.

Becky, our class salutatorian, commented wistfully, "Wouldn't
it be nice if we could get together more often, not just every five
years?"

"Why can't we?" I ventured, feeling relieved that I wasn't the
only melancholy one. "We could meet once a month and at least
eat together." "Yeah," echoed several locals, including Buddy, a
first-time participator in the reunions.

Weeks later, the first gathering proved awkward as conversation competed with the café's commotion. Finally, we found a place that worked: Demetre's Restaurant offered us a cozy private room.

Only one other couple showed up the next time. I morosely cupped my chin in my hands and contemplated "what next?" Our get-togethers had fizzled. My mind whirred, *How does one motivate without nagging?* "Maybe it's not meant to be," Lee suggested. I glared at him.

Write! My palm slapped the tabletop. "I'm gonna start a newsletter!"

The first 59ers newsletters were solo flights, each taking three entire days as I composed the text; copied, collated, stuffed, and addressed envelopes by hand; and stamped and mailed all 105 letters. The issues reported folksy local news and gossip fodder from Demetre's gatherings, sandwiched with essays and my eternal message: relationships are the best thing going—let's make a difference! At our next dinner, teamwork kicked in when somebody passed the hat for donations to underwrite the venture. My gut instinct said that giving voluntarily, requiring nothing in return, was the catalyst that we needed to enjoy one another.

Amazing advances resulted. At one meeting, Alinda, God bless her, said, "Come to my tax office, and I'll run and collate the newsletters and cover the cost." "I can do the address labels on my computer," offered Phyllis. Somebody else chimed in, "Bring the letters with you here to Demetre's so we can all stuff envelopes."

"Hey!" suggested Betty. "Let's all get theater tickets to see *Grease.* I'll order for us."

"We're as near each other as the phone," I reminded them, handing out rosters. Buddy, now an avid regular, kept us in stitches with his endless quips. Our after-Thanksgiving bash was a hit. We pooled all our leftovers and feasted together to ward off post-holiday blahs.

By now, volunteers Erlene, Phyllis, Brenda, and Mary Sue

helped call locals for our gatherings. The newsletter added a pro-
files section, featuring a classmate per issue. Profound stories of
courage and spirit emerged. Roger, a minister, had miraculously
survived not one, but two, near-fatal heart attacks. Brenda's
stroke should have killed or disabled her, but she fully recovered.
Judy is now the Honorable City Councilwoman. Erlene and
Patsy, who had each lost a precious daughter, inspired us all with
their grit, faith, and serenity. Marlene had raised her girls alone,
and gone on to receive the Governor's Order of the Palmetto
Award for civic contributions. The stories of our classmates are
endless.

Reactions were immediate. Danny, whom I remembered as
that cute red-haired football player with a vibrant smile, called
from Maine to thank me for keeping him in touch with the old
gang and revealed a longing to see everybody. Letters, cards, and
E-mails arrived from many others.

I daily scanned the obituary column. Locals congregated at funeral homes to comfort classmates whose parents or mates had
passed on. Days later, the bereaved received a love-gift check
from the 59ers for "a quiet dinner out for two" during their difficult days of sorrow. The Kitty Fund miraculously burgeoned
through it all.

My phone rang constantly with reports of happenings. Prayer
became a paramount link to one another's rainy days. We all
grieved together when Willie, a classmate, died suddenly. We
prayed for Jud when his banking position was phased out and re-
joiced with him when he found another job. I had my first book
signing, and my pals came, each of them as excited as I was. Before long, other alumni and retired teachers began dropping by
Demetre's to join us.

At one dinner, Ronnie and Joan declared it was time for a
cookout. The teamwork preceding that event still amazes me,
from the folksy phone brigade—headed by Buddy, Jerry, and
Charlie—to the sturdy tables now swaying beneath enough cov-

ered dishes to feed an army. The guys grilled, and we all ate, visited, and lingered long afterward, comfortable and at ease, listening to old '50s tunes.

We all piled in vans and cars one weekend for a trip to Myrtle Beach for a '50s concert with Fabian and, in the flesh, Bobby Rydell.

Our fortieth high school reunion marked five years since our regular get-togethers. We all strolled down memory lane, the same halls we'd shared as teenagers, and played the "remember when" game.

That magical night, Kathy and James met again for the first time in four decades. I watched them dancing together as they had done so often years ago. Newly widowed, Kathy tearfully thanked me for the 59ers love-gift, a music box that played "You Light Up My Life." Two years earlier, she'd come to a restaurant for what she thought was a private birthday celebration. The gang all yelled "Surprise!" followed by misty hugs. Kathy, the still-lovely ex-cheerleader, stood up after dinner and said, "I've shunned our reunions because I didn't want you to see my extra pounds and gray hairs. But"—she choked up—"I'm so glad you ambushed me!" I now blinked away tears as well. Tonight, here she was with us. And I recalled how James, divorced for many years, had declared himself a loner during our long-distance phone chats. I sighed, pleased that they were enjoying the evening together.

Our Demetre's gatherings grew more and more warm and relaxed, the ambience like that of family at mealtime.

Last week, Kathy's phone number showed up on my caller ID. Concerned, I called her. "We wanted all of you to know that James and I are getting married next week," was her breathless announcement. "Ever since we dated as seniors," she added softly, "James confessed he's carried my picture in his billfold." My joy was indescribable. "Thanks for sharing this most special moment with me—with us," I said, holding back a sob.

In that moment, I flashed on Kathy's birthday after-dinner speech, when she had said, "The great thing about being together now is that what you see is what you get—middle-age baggage and all. Hey! There's nothing to prove." She had wiped away a tear. "Y'know, guys, relationships really *are* the best thing going."

Ironically, by sharing all these experiences, we've rendered ourselves ageless. Our time spent together tethers us to our former selves before spouses and offspring. Together, we reclaim a joyful, carefree thread of our past and braid it to our present. Knotted together, we really *do* make a difference.

EMILY SUE HARVEY

WINIFRED'S
LEGACY OF LOVE

People like Winifred Austin Fisher made me nervous. As the director of fundraising at a large urban hospital, I would be eternally grateful to the woman whose last will and testament lay scattered across my desk, but at the same time, her lifestyle frightened me. Perhaps because it reflected my own too closely.

Born in Hyde Park, Massachusetts, in 1910, Winifred was the only child of Austin and Mary Fisher. A steamfitter, her father died in 1925 of scarlet fever, leaving little in the way of assets. Two years later, Winifred broke with the tradition of the day by gaining employment as a bookkeeper. At seventeen, she was not only a "working woman" but had the added distinction of being the sole support of her mother.

For the next fifty years, Winifred spent a good part of her life crunching numbers. She never married, had no children, and after her mother died in 1952, lived alone. At the time of her own death, Winifred had no living relatives, and she bequeathed nearly $1 million to local charities. The largest portion was left to our hospital.

"Ah, Winnie," I sighed, looking through her file, "why didn't you spend some of that money on yourself?" From what I could ascertain, her last address was a three-room apartment in a four-story walk-up. And the building itself was located in one of the least desirable sections of the city.

Several days later I met with her attorney, a distinguished el-

derly gentleman, to discuss a fitting memorial for our benefac-
tor. "She was a very private person, mild-mannered but deci-
sive," he recalled. "She knew exactly what she wanted. She was
conscientious, diligent, thrifty, and rarely indulged herself. She
had a deep feeling for charitable causes, particularly in the health
care field. Use her money wisely."

But who was Winifred Austin Fisher? I wanted to scream at
the lawyer. What were her dreams? Her fears? Was she ever in
love? Did she wear purple? Or incredible hats? Had she ever seen
the Eiffel Tower? Or travel to Tibet? Did she sing in the shower?
Or walk barefoot in the park? Who was she? I wanted to know.

Unfortunately, I'd probably never find out. And while the timing of her death prevented me from obtaining any personal information, the timing of her bequest could not have been better.
The hospital had recently undertaken a major building cam-
paign, and thanks to Winifred, the project would now be completed on time and within budget. After speaking with her
attorney, we decided to apply a large portion of her contribution
to the pediatric emergency area.

As a former public relations professional, I pulled out all the
stops to make Winifred's donation a media blitz. At the dedication ceremony, reporters were out in force, and one major news
station in Manhattan sent a film crew. The following day, every
newspaper printed her picture beneath a banner headline reading "HEAVEN SENT."

While I was pleased that Winifred had finally received the
recognition she so much deserved, nothing could compare to
the way I felt when I discovered that the first patient treated in
the new pediatrics area was a little boy named Austin. A benevo-
lent force was at work somewhere, and I sensed that Winifred
was pleased that we had used her money wisely.

But Winifred's legacy to me was so much more than medical
equipment, bricks, mortar, and a lucrative bottom line. I thought

about her constantly that first year, and began to make subtle changes in my own life "in the name of Winnie."

That year, I bought a new wardrobe in vibrant colors, relinquishing my traditional beige and navy. I booked a trip to Paris (solo like Lucky Lindy!), forsaking the Jersey shore. I began to investigate several charities, and initiated a program for women with cancer. Later that fall, contemplating a career move, I attended a seminar on eldercare. The presenter was a rakish-looking man whose command of the language captivated the audience. During the break, we began a conversation over the coffeepot.

"You work at the hospital, don't you?" he asked. Without waiting for my reply, he continued, "I recognize you from that dedication ceremony last year. You did a great job. Winnie would have loved it. I knew her, you know. I used to visit her quite often. How did you know she loved children?"

Looking into the eyes of the man who was to become my husband, I answered, "I just did. But can you tell me, did she like purple hats?"

BARBARA DAVEY

LOVE ALWAYS, MOM

I can still remember the overcast day of April 8, 1992, in Dallas as if it were yesterday. In spite of the gloomy day my heart was filled with joy and excitement as I was preparing for my trip to Arizona to visit my boyfriend, Neal. We had met four months earlier at a mutual friend's house.

Since that time, Neal and I had developed a very close and caring relationship. We would take turns visiting each other, since we lived miles apart. Neal had phoned earlier that day to remind me to bring my college transcripts to Arizona with me. It had been almost ten years since my last college course, but I was considering returning to complete my degree. As I pulled out my briefcase from under my desk, I got a good laugh over all the dust it had collected. I was sure it had been under my desk untouched for at least six years. As I reached in the side pocket, the first thing I pulled out was an old florist's card. Once again I started to laugh, wondering what dysfunctional relationship this card was from. Who knows how many there had been. I had just about given up hopes of ever finding Mr. Right. As I opened the card a warm feeling and a big smile came over me as I read, "Love Always, Mom."

I sat there for a minute reflecting on my mother and our special relationship. She always knew how to cheer me up. She would send me cards or flowers to brighten my day if I was feeling down, and other times just to say I love you.

Mom also had a great sense of humor, and as a child I could

always get myself out of trouble by making her laugh. I'll never forget the time she was so mad at me she chased me all over the backyard with a wooden spoon. By the time she caught up with me, we were both laughing so hard that we forgot why I was in trouble. Or the many times we would go out to dinner together, and I would return to our table to find several men waiting to meet my mother's (her words) "beautiful, smart, and very eligible daughter."

Serious times came to mind, too. Once I contracted a deadly virus and spent two weeks in the hospital with my mother never leaving my side. And, the many hours we spent sharing our hopes and dreams for the future. I always felt secure knowing my mother would always be there for me. She truly wanted the best for her three daughters. That's why I was so excited about our dinner together a few nights earlier when I told her all about Neal, and that I really felt like this relationship was the one. I promised her that on Neal's next visit to Dallas she would get to meet him.

As I looked at my watch it was 10:15 A.M. I had just enough time to run a few last-minute errands in preparation for my trip to Arizona and be back before my staff's lunch breaks began. I placed the florist's card on my desk. When I started to leave, the phone in my office rang. I picked up the phone, and a weird sensation swept over me. It was as if time had stopped. I could hear my older sister on the phone sobbing. She told me Mom was dead. I felt paralyzed. How could this be? She was so full of life and laughter just a few nights ago. I hung up the phone and quickly raced to my parents' home. I had to see my mom before they took her away.

As I entered her room, my beautiful mother lay lifeless in her bed. I crawled in next to her and just held her in my arms. I knew it would be the last time I ever got to kiss or hold her again. The laughter, joy, and security I knew were now gone. I can't remember how long I held her while making promises to God so he'd give her back to me for just ten more minutes. I still had so many things I needed to tell her.

As I lay crying, I remembered the florist's card I had found. Now I had to know exactly what time my mom had died. I was told she had died somewhere around ten that morning. I raced back to my office to get the florist's card, knowing that this must have been my mother's way of letting me know she would always love me. To my surprise, the card was nowhere to be found. My coworkers assured me that no one had been in my office. Now I was sure that my mother had truly sent me a message to let me know that she will always love me.

Unfortunately, my mother never got to meet Neal—who later became my husband. This year we celebrated the birth of our daughter, whom we named after my mother, Kelsey Joyce. I know my mother's spirit and our special bond will live on through my daughter and myself. I plan on doing all the things for her that my mom did for me to make me feel special. I will send her cards and flowers and sign them, "Love Always, Mom."

KIM DIXON WALDMAN

A CHARMED LIFE

The only gift I remember receiving on my fortieth birthday is the one my mother gave me. She passed on the silver charm bracelet my father had given her during their early years of marriage. Dad delighted in the concept of a charm bracelet because it simplified gift giving for years to come. No endless searching for the perfect gift for anniversaries or birthdays, just one trip to the jewelry store to choose the perfect charm to honor the important events in their lives together.

Growing up, this charm bracelet was a constant source of entertainment and fascination for me. When Mom dressed for parties, she adorned her wrist with it. As she walked out the door, the way it jingled reminded me of fairy music, and I remember listening for that sound when she came home at night, long after I'd been tucked into bed.

I loved to spin that bracelet around her wrist and listen to it sparkle with sound. As she waited for my father to whisk her off to a party, I sat close to her and ran my hand over the fabric of her fancy dress, became intoxicated with the smell of her Tabu perfume, and wondered if I'd ever be as beautiful as her.

It's funny to think of it now, but she was just about forty at the time. Forty looked young and vibrant on my mother. Sitting on the couch, waiting, we played a storytelling game. I'd select a charm, then beg her to tell me the story behind it. One of my favorite charms was a miniature ring, representing my father's proposal at her parents' home in York, Pennsylvania, during the Christmas of 1952. Mom refused to see the ring before saying yes, thinking it might influence her decision. Several days later, during an evening walk, she agreed to marry my father. He gave her a sparkling emerald-cut diamond ring.

The minute she finished the story, my mind whirled, envisioning my parents courting, getting to know each other, and deciding to marry. I imagined what they wore and how they looked. Their life before me was a marvelous mystery.

As a little girl, I glossed over the part of Mom's story about thinking over Dad's proposal for a few days. It didn't register until I was in a similar situation. When my boyfriend proposed, I initially felt isolated by doubt and confusion. I remember standing at the corner of Cuyler and Southport in Chicago, walking with my mother during a visit, and talking about my indecision. She said, "You remind me of me." And the story of the ring charm unfolded all over again. As she repeated it for me, I heard it in a whole new way and no longer felt alone.

Tonight, as I prepare to go out for the evening with my husband, I spin Mom's charm bracelet, the tinkle of memories making music against my own wrist. Each charm is a tribute to my mother's life and the milestones she's passed over the years. I'm proud to be the keeper of such history and humbled by the empty spaces that remain for me to add my own memories.

MARI PAT VARGA

OH, SO SWEET

I chose to marry on my mother and father's thirty-ninth wedding anniversary, in April with spring flowers in bloom, birds singing, and trees just beginning to bud.

Like most brides, I wanted everything to be perfect, including my hair. It needed to be able to withstand a small tornado, if necessary, and I left that task up to Paula, owner of a newly opened hair salon in town. Paula's grandmother, Angela Backes, walked in and sat down to wait for her appointment while Paula worked her magic on me. We talked for a bit, and when she realized I was getting married that day, her face brightened.

"Well, my wedding anniversary is tomorrow!" she said.

"Really?" I asked in surprise.

"We married April 29, 1931," she began. "Those first years were rough. We were farmers, and money definitely wasn't one of our luxuries," she continued. Then, with a smile on her face and a twinkle in her eye, Mrs. Backes told me about her first wedding anniversary.

I could tell that this particular memory was one she would always hold dear. With a look of fond recollection, she said, "You know, we were barely getting by, so I sure didn't expect a gift for our anniversary." Then she laughed a bit, and said, "I was so surprised when he walked up to me and handed me a bouquet of freshly bloomed sweet Williams that he had picked for me." They are beautiful wildflowers in shades of purple that bloom in early spring. Their scent is as wonderful as their beauty. She thought it was so sweet of him.

As years passed, he continued this tradition, even after money was plentiful. For their fiftieth wedding anniversary, a celebration was planned but had to be rescheduled. Unfortunately, Mrs. Backes had to be hospitalized during that time. She knew the tradition well and wondered if he would embarrass her by bringing wildflowers to the hospital instead of purchased flowers. She said, "I wondered what the nurses would think."

Shuffling slowly down the corridors and into her room, with the aroma of wildflowers filling the air, he carried one of the largest bouquets of sweet Williams he had ever given her. Everyone told her how sweet they thought it was, including her nurses. At his age, buying flowers would have probably been easier than picking them, but it was his way of showing he cared—and in a beautiful way.

I felt a special connection with her as she told me the story. It was the same flower that my soon-to-be husband had given me on his first visit to my home. Traveling by motorcycle, he saw them by the roadside, stopped to pick some, and placed them in one of the saddlebags. It was later in the day when he remembered, or had the nerve to give them to me. The delicate petals were extremely wilted; but the thought still seemed so sweet.

Fred and Angela Backes celebrated a total of sixty-one years of marriage. They were blessed with two children, plus grandchildren and great-grandchildren. Mrs. Backes passed away in June of 1992, but on April 29, 1993, Fred did as he had every year since they married. He gave her a beautiful bouquet of sweet Williams, only this time he placed them on her grave.

JENNY KREFTMEYER ALTHEN

X
DANCING WITH ANGELS

Angels are pure thoughts from God, winged with Truth and Love.

MARY BAKER EDDY

My work is noisy, but my life is quiet.
TINA TURNER

WHEN INTERPRETATION COUNTS

When it comes to my dreams, I always yearn to know their significance. I keep a dream journal to get a sneak peek at my psyche before she's censored by rationality. I usually don't pay too much attention to violent dreams, or necessarily trust that dream premonitions are accurate. My dreams have elicited every feeling from fear to elation, but none has had as lasting an effect as "the bus dream."

One night, I dreamt I was on my way to the bus stop across busy Kennedy Boulevard in Jersey City. The day was shot with tree green from the park across the street. The neighborhood pharmacy kept sentry on the corner, and a ceiling of sheer blue capped the city. As I stepped into the street, the light began flashing, "Don't Walk . . . Don't Walk," but I knew I had ample time before the light changed. I hurried across, my eye on the bus stop on the other side, and with no warning, a bus hit and crushed me between it and another car!

I fought to get out of the dream and open my eyes. By the time I did, I felt as though I'd just run a marathon. Sweat trickled between my breasts, and my heart pounded so hard I could barely catch my breath. I clicked on the bedside lamp, opened my dream journal, and paused, pen in hand. After a few minutes, I just shook my head and wrote, "Strange."

The following morning left me no time to ponder the bus dream's meaning. A meeting across town had me flying through my hair and makeup routine. By the time I got to the panty hose, I was already fifteen minutes behind. If I got the bus connections right, I could still make it on time. The briefcase strap dug into my shoulder as I half ran toward the bus stop. As I approached the corner, I saw the traffic in the cross lanes rolling to a stop. The light was about to change, and I'd have to push it now or wait another few minutes to cross. Bus 88 pulled up on the other side of the street and that made my decision. I darted into the intersection, waving to catch the bus driver's attention before he pulled away from the curb without me. Suddenly, a nauseous feeling brought me up short in the middle of the intersection. I felt I'd been here before. The day was shot with tree green from the park across the street. The neighborhood pharmacy kept sentry on the corner, and a ceiling of sheer blue capped the city. The light before me flashed, "Don't Walk . . . Don't Walk." Bus 88, my bus, came careening past me, out of control, through the red light and crashed into a car, causing a five-car pileup. No one was hurt, but I knew that if I'd continued crossing I'd have been crushed between the bus and the car, just like in my dream.

I no longer cared about the time and walked a lot slower, enjoying the miracle of life's frailty and generosity. I arrived at my meeting very late, but no real loss, because I finally knew what to jot down in my dream journal:

Pay Attention
Trust God
Dream

JUDY TORRES

GOLD LAMÉ FAIRY DUST

I *lost my mom in 1988 to leukemia. She was gorgeous,* glamorous, and a vibrant woman. Even though I was grateful that her illness lasted only five weeks, her death gave no warning and was quite a shock for me. I missed her terribly and thought of all the things I would have liked to do with her and say to her. It was hard to get through holidays and special events without her.

She was a special mother. She taught me to believe in God and miracles and fairy tales and all magical things under heaven. Her grandmother had been what they called a medium. She spoke to spirits at night by the fireplace while my mother as a small girl huddled in the hallway with her three sisters, giggling as they peeked around the corner to watch her. This intuitive gift was passed on to my mom. For instance, I remember my mom knowing the moment that John F. Kennedy was shot. She was home vacuuming when she suddenly knew he had died. She shut the vacuum off and turned the television on to discover the tragedy on the news. Another time, her father's spirit appeared at the foot of her bed moments after he had passed away. Things like this frequently occurred to my mom and seemed quite natural to me as a small child.

When I was four or five, I remember feeling the presence of my guardian angel when I said my prayers at night. I felt comforted by my angel's presence, and would hold out my hand for her to hold. I was certain that I felt the pressure of her hand wrapping around mine. I had a lot of intuition growing up. I would often finish someone's sentence, or know who was calling when the phone rang, but I never thought of myself as having the same gift as my mother, and certainly not my great-grand-mother's. As I grew up, I lost my connection with my spiritual awareness and became distracted with everyday life and all its struggles.

A year after my mom's death, I started writing letters to her on my computer. I had so many things I wanted to say to her and ask her, and my letters became an exercise in healing my grief. There was a part of me, however, that hoped she would find ways to answer me back. I didn't know how, but I was always looking for signs. For quite a while, I didn't notice anything. But, as my letters continued, coincidences started to happen that I thought could be messages from her. I began to pay attention to them. These messages were subtle and yet seemed very power-ful each time they occurred. There would be a chance phone call from an old acquaintance with a catch phrase my mom used to use, or a book I happened to pick up that fell open to a passage that contained an answer to a question I had asked my mom, or a movie I went to see with a special message seemingly meant just for me. As much as I wanted to completely believe in all this "magical" communication, I had to admit it all could be just coincidence.

Then, something happened to me one beautiful spring day when I least expected it.

My husband, Brian, and I sailed our yacht to Catalina Island for the annual Conservancy Ball held in the beautiful 1920s art deco Casino Ball Room. Men decked out in black tuxedos and women in beautiful long gowns carefully climb off their yachts into little rubber dinghies to putter up to the casino for an evening of big band dancing and silent auction bidding. It's a yearly event we never miss!

We took our friends Rob and Karen this time, and side-tied to a power yacht with four other friends in the Avalon Harbor.

Saturday afternoon, I took a short nap forward in the V-berth. When I awoke, I was staring into my mother's diamond engagement ring that I always wear. I had never seen it shining so brightly. It was casting prisms of light that covered the entire forward cabin ceiling. I felt my mom's presence strongly. I poked my head up through the forward hatch, and there in front of us, bobbing on a mooring, was a boat named *Blanche* . . . my mother's name. *My mom . . . she must be here!* She loved glamour, and this was a black tie event. I felt excited.

Around 4:30 P.M., I slipped into my long red evening gown to have early cocktails aboard our neighbor's yacht. I pulled out a little gold beaded evening bag that used to belong to my mother. I opened it to tuck my lipstick inside and was surprised to discover my mom's beautiful evening-length gold lamé gloves. They had to be at least forty years old, but looked in mint condition.

With a little urging from my husband and Karen, I decided to wear them.

My mom's hands were slightly smaller than mine, so Karen helped me wriggle into them and fasten the little carved brass buttons at the wrist.

While balancing a glass of champagne, I hoisted my long gown, climbed over the boat railing, and stepped aboard our neighbor's yacht to join our friends.

Someone complimented me on my red dress, especially its pretty gold shimmer. I looked down, and lo and behold, I was covered with gold lamé. Then, in perfect rhythm, Brian stood up with gold lamé all over his black tuxedo jacket. Then, Karen held up the palms of her hands, revealing a luster of gold lamé. Then, Rob stood up. The front of his black pants glistened with gold lamé. Everyone erupted in uproarious laughter.

"Wait a minute," I protested. "I didn't go anywhere near Rob. It was Karen. She has it all over her hands!"

They teased me anyway, unmercifully. We all laughed so hard,

I thought I would split my dress open. Then, everyone wanted to be "gold laméd." I touched the guys' lapels and the gals' shoulders, and by the end of the evening everyone had been "laméd" by Mother's gold fairy dust.

There were way too many coincidences this time to doubt my mother's presence. The prisms of light reflected from her ring, her sense of glamour, her sense of humor, the boat bearing her name. What more validation did I need? I marveled at the brilliant procession of events that let me know in no uncertain terms that she was indeed there communicating with me.

The more I pay attention to the signs in front of me, the stronger my connection becomes with my mom and the more in touch I am with the wondrous realms of spirit. I used to consider this awareness a gift, but have come to realize that it is a natural process. I only need to remove my doubts and allow the veil to part that separates me from the spirit world and those I love. Then, just watch and listen.

TANNIS BENEDICT

A HOLY ENCOUNTER

*S*everal years ago, I attended a lecture and slide show on angels at the American Museum of Natural History in New York City. The lecture traced the belief in angels, in both art and literature, from ancient to modern times. It also included testimonies from people who felt that they had personally communicated with these supernatural beings.

One woman claimed a very special relationship with Saint Michael, the Archangel. She said that he spoke to her on a regular basis and told her how disappointed he was that so few humans contacted him for help. According to her, Michael desperately wanted to be friends with everyone on earth. Naturally, I had some doubts about these messages from this famous angel, and I even snickered a bit under my breath.

Just the same, I decided to put the theory to a test. I needed some help fast! For two weeks, my apartment keys had been missing. One of the "keys" was a photo ID card key that let me into the forty-five-story skyscraper apartment building where I lived. This was causing me great inconvenience, because every time I entered the building, I had to sign in. If the key was not found soon, I would have to be rephotographed and issued a new card key at some expense. Also, since I didn't have a second set of keys, I had to leave the door to my apartment open, which is not a good idea in New York City.

I had searched all over my apartment for the keys; high upon closet shelves and low, underneath beds and couches, thinking my cats had hidden them somewhere. I looked in purses, bookcases, and even in the refrigerator, but to no avail. My keys were nowhere to be found at home or at work, and I worried that they were permanently lost.

So, on the night after the lecture, I prayed to Michael, asking him to find my keys *immediately!* I fell asleep laughing to myself: Ha! Ha!

The next morning I woke up, swung my legs over the side of the bed, put my feet on the floor, and there, in front of my toes, were my keys! Chills went up and down my spine. My reasoning mind told me that my cats had, at last, dragged them from some secret hiding place, but my spirit knew that my prayers had been answered.

Humbled and slightly frightened, I got down on my knees and thanked my new friend Michael, the Archangel.

FRANCINE M. STOREY

Faith is the very first thing you should pack in a hope chest.
SARAH BAN BREATHNACH

TIMELY MATTER

When I was nine, I remember us kids teasing Dad unmercifully the night before his birthday. My eldest brother ribbed him playfully, "Dad, we thought you were old when you turned forty! But forty-three, that's *really* old!"

Mom planned the usual cake-and-present celebration that we all looked forward to, but it never happened. A few hours after Dad went to sleep that night, he awoke in excruciating pain. Mom ran for a cool compress and called for help as Dad went into a seizure. A blood clot in his brain had ruptured.

Three days later, Mom made the heart-wrenching decision to turn off his life support system. We were all devastated at Dad's death. He was such a treasure: a school administrator, a local politician, an active member of the church, but most importantly, a devoted husband and father. Ice skating in the winter, picnics and my brothers' ball games in the summer, and long rides in the country that ended with ice cream are some of my fondest memories of time spent with Dad.

Following in Mom and Dad's footsteps, I too wanted to create the kind of loving relationship they had shared, so it was no surprise to anyone when I became engaged.

My fiancé and I were both living in the New England area, far from our families. As soon as we announced our plan to wed where we lived, certain family members balked. They wanted the wedding in our hometown. I started to feel incredibly guilty about our decision. A million worries coursed through my mind. Were we being selfish? Would anyone come to the wedding? Did the entire family feel the same way, but they just weren't admitting it?

My fiancé assured me that having the wedding in New England was the right thing to do. He reminded me about what had ultimately been the deciding factor—the church. We both loved St. Anne's. We attended mass there each Sunday, and I cherished those quiet moments of prayer that brought us closer.

During the stressful months before the wedding, I often skipped lunch to visit the little white church on the winding country road. In serene silence, I sat in one of the front pews, closed my eyes, and whispered the prayers I had repeated hundreds of times before. Then I talked to my dad.

When I was nine years old, Mom had promised me that Dad was an angel looking down from above. When I needed him, all I had to do was speak to him as if he were right in front of me. I told Dad about my week at work, the latest family anecdotes, and often asked him for wisdom, strength, and support.

One afternoon, though, I stopped by the church and didn't bother reciting my usual litany. I barely made it to my favorite pew before I began to sob. I felt alone, confused, and scared by my impending wedding and all the family politics. Teary-eyed and exhausted from sadness, I knelt and asked Dad for strength and a sign that he was there with me.

Suddenly, the church bells chimed. They rang bold, clear sounds. My heart leapt to my throat. My mind raced. *Is this my sign?* I wondered. I quickly dismissed the thought and reasoned the chiming was just the huge antique bell on the clock tower bursting forth its hourly reminder. I hastily gathered up my handbag and sweater. Since I'd left the office at 12:15 P.M., I barely had enough time to make it back to work before my 1:15 P.M. deadline.

My car clock was on the fritz, so I really didn't know what time it was as I pondered the reaction from my boss to my tardiness. When I finally reached the office, I was frazzled from my traffic-ridden trip through town and positive I was late. He stood in the office as I entered, and my stomach sank. "Sorry I'm late. Traffic was—" I began.

"You're back early!" he said. "What's the rush on a beautiful day like today?"

"Early?" I said, stunned.

He shoved his watch right up to my nose. It read one minute to one. I turned to the clock on the wall behind me. It confirmed his watch. Seconds later, the large timepiece atop City Hall sounded the hour. I quietly smiled to myself for the rest of the day.

I have been married for over a year now. I still visit the little church and have my heart-to-heart talks with Dad when the pressures of life are overbearing. One serene afternoon, during a brief exchange with the priest, he enlightened me on the church's history—and proudly mentioned that the church clock has kept perfect time for over twenty-five years.

TARA GLENNON OTT

ANGELS IN TOW

Both *seventeen, my friend Tim and I had a lot in* common. On a frosty, late autumn night, we ran into each other at a high school party. Like most parties in the 1970s, this one had air that was thick with smoke and cheap alcohol. Tim and I discussed friends, family, and musician Rick Wakemen, and around 10:00 P.M. he confided in me that he felt sick.

We decided to share a pot of coffee at a local café. I wasn't much of a drinker, so I figured I could safely drive his dad's old car. We jogged to the coupe on the frost-covered grass and prayed the cold engine would start. When we neared the aged, white Chevy, Tim insisted on taking the wheel. He assured me he was okay. For the most part he was, and like most seventeen-year-olds, we felt immortal.

He carefully turned the key in the ignition, and the car stubbornly growled into submission. We took off down the pretty residential street. Tim said he knew a shortcut to the café. As we drove, I noticed the houses were disappearing and deserted wooded areas engulfed the road. With full confidence in my dear friend, we continued to chat about the usual.

Suddenly, Tim swerved to avoid an animal, and we slipped into a ditch. He put the heap in reverse and gunned it. We finally landed in a deeper ditch on the other side of the forsaken, desolate road. He politely and calmly apologized as he crawled out of the door. He hit the ground flat on his face. I chuckled until I realized the severity of our situation. The car was slanted and unstable as it rested on the land's natural incline. Fortunately, we'd missed a row of trees—a miracle by itself. They seemed to look at us with disapproval. I reviewed the situation; all I could think about was my friends, my family, and a telephone. Each was out of our reach. Tim said he needed to get to a bathroom. The closest one, of course, was the woods. Fearing he would pass out in the city's forest, I asked him to keep talking to me.

As I waited for him to return, I listened to the awesome singing of the remaining crickets, birds, and other creatures on this frigid fall night. I could smell fumes inside the car from burnt radiator fluid. By the time Tim returned, I was feeling very anxious. We decided to walk to a phone and call for help. I made a quick exit from the car. Gravity ruled and the door slammed arrogantly.

Out of nowhere, a warm light traveled toward us on the winding, secluded road. We waved, jumped, and screamed when the driver came into view. Much to our surprise, it was a young couple in a tow truck. The nicely dressed young man hopped out of the truck to see if we were okay and then dragged the Chevy to the road. We rummaged through our pockets for our coffee money to use as partial payment for the tow. We knew this was going to be an expensive rescue for two high school kids.

We turned our heads to thank him and give him our parents' names and numbers for reimbursement. But when we looked up, the truck was gone. Where did they go? We looked at each other in surprise, then dashed for the car, praying that the beast had at least one more burst of energy to get us home. Tim once again turned the key, and mysteriously, without hesitation, the engine purred easily.

We quietly rode home without the coffee. Nevertheless, it was a sobering experience. Neither of us discussed this event until years later. We both agreed it was one of those times we were touched by angels in tow.

ANTIONETTE VIGLIATURO ISHMAEL

THE PRESENCE OF AN ANGEL

"**G**od, please send an angel to be with Daddy today," I humbly asked, down on my knees in our motel room.

It had been over two years since my heart was shattered by the news of my father's terminal illness. After that day, I spent as much time as possible with Daddy.

My twenty-third wedding anniversary arrived, and my husband planned a weekend getaway at a quaint and familiar resort in Stone Mountain, Georgia. There was a chill in the air, and Christmas was only two weeks away. I looked so forward to this trip. Everywhere we went, however, remembrances of Daddy entered my mind.

The last time that I visited the resort, my father was with us. As we were sightseeing during our visit, I saw Daddy's smile. At breakfast, I heard his laughter. As we strolled through the historical plantation houses, I felt Daddy's tender touch as he put his arm around my neck a few years earlier. Oh, how I missed his touch, and how I wished that he could hug me just one more time.

My husband knew that I needed a break from the stress. After quite a few years of marriage, I had the opportunity to spend two nights in a hotel bridal suite. I felt so honored and so loved by him.

When he went down the hallway to get ice around lunchtime, I knelt down and thanked God for the opportunity to be there, for my wonderful husband, and even for the bittersweet memories I associated with the resort. I further thanked Him for giving me a loving father for over forty-three years. I closed with a request. I asked God to send an angel to take care of Daddy while I was away from him.

When my husband came back inside, I closed my prayer. My heart was lighter, and I felt more refreshed. An unusual feeling of peace fell around me. Our afternoon was busy, as we shopped and searched for souvenirs and Christmas presents for everyone on our shopping list. Together we laughed, enjoyed an early dinner, and returned to the resort to enjoy the seasonal festivities of the evening.

We went back to our room to call my mother to check on Daddy. We talked for several minutes, and just as we were about to hang up, she said, "Hold on, Nancy. Let me tell you something unusual that happened at the nursing home today."

She told me about a woman who visited Daddy. She explained how she went to get some lunch and when she returned, the head nurse met her at the front door.

"There's a stranger in your husband's room," the nurse said to Mom. "We've been keeping an eye out because we've never seen her before." My mother quickly walked to Daddy's room. A young lady was praying with him. My mother stood quietly until the woman finished. At that point, she turned to look at my mother. She was smiling warmly.

"Hi," she said. "I know you don't know me, but God sent me here. I live across town. As I was pulling out of my driveway, God spoke to me. He told me to come here. Since I didn't know where I was going, I allowed Him to guide me. He brought me straight to this nursing home parking lot."

When she got out of her car, she said that she asked God to show her which room to visit. "As I was walking down the hall and came to this room, He told me that this was the place. So I stopped. I hope you don't mind."

"Of course not," my mother responded, "you're welcome here anytime."

She hugged my mother and started to leave. "By the way," she said, "God said to tell you that everything is going to be fine." With those words, she left the room, the building, and our lives.

I was quiet as my mother shared these events with me over the phone.

"Did this happen between twelve-thirty P.M. and one P.M. today?" I asked.

"It was about one when I got back," she replied. "Why do you ask?"

"Because that was the time that I asked God to send an angel to take care of Daddy," I replied.

"Do you think she was an angel, Nancy?" my mother asked.

"Do you have any better explanation?" I responded.

"No, I don't," she replied. While Mom's voice sounded puzzled, I knew in my heart that this angel was the answer to my prayer. Her presence assured me that God was listening as I prayed that day.

The remainder of our trip was delightful. I returned to the nursing home a few days later, and Daddy smiled as I entered his room. He had not smiled at me for a while, so I was very grateful. As he reached out to me with his feeble hand, I placed my arms around him and gave him a hug.

When I left his room that day, I had the assurance that no matter what happens, everything is going to be fine. Like my husband, God knew I needed a break and a time of renewal, both physically and spiritually. It turned out to be the most wonderful trip my husband and I have ever taken together.

I have found that sometimes God speaks to our hearts, but at other times He speaks loudly and clearly through the presence of an angel.

NANCY B. GIBBS

You can't be brave if you've only had
wonderful things happen to you.
<small>MARY TYLER MOORE</small>

FOLLOWING
THE WHISPERS

Five years ago, I left the Pacific Northwest with everything I owned packed in my Toyota, not knowing for sure where I would land nor how I would live. I had $2,700 to my name. It was one of those dark-nights-of-the-soul times in my life when I felt completely empty after yet another relationship failed.

It was the third time for me, and I felt like I'd lost everything and everyone important in my life—three families, old friends, my business—and most assuredly myself. My best friend was involved with my soon-to-be ex-husband, which made me want to leave Oregon since there was no chance of my surviving this latest life crisis while being close by.

The Southwest held appeal to me, yet without a job to go to or savings to draw on, relocating there seemed impossible. A few remaining friends thought otherwise. They saw possibilities for me that I could not see. One suggested a garage sale and fund-raising party to pay for the journey. A few weeks later, all I had left to my name was my car, my clothes, my TV, and my computer, plus the $2,700 raised from the sale of my things. I planned the trip so that

I could stay with people I knew the first few days, then once I left Los Angeles, I would be on my own. This was the first time in my life that I wasn't with either my parents, or a husband, or a friend. Just me.

I was never so scared in my entire life as the day I left on my journey. The first sign that I was "being taken care of" was the twenty or so hawks soaring above my car as I drove the first leg of my trip. Hawks had become a powerful symbol for me and had come to represent my intuition. It was a sign to me that I was doing the right thing, even though I was terrified.

The first stop on my journey was southern Oregon, where I stayed with two friends. When I told them I was heading toward Arizona and New Mexico, one called her mother's friend, Mary Alice, in Albuquerque. She was looking for a house sitter in three weeks, and I agreed to do it.

On the way, I did some things I'd always wanted to do—like drive the Highway 101 coast road through Big Sur and on to Los Angeles. It was as spectacular as I had imagined it to be. It was only after I left Los Angeles that I came face-to-face with what I'd done and where I was in my sorry excuse for a life.

I sobbed my way through the Mojave Desert on my way to Arizona. I was literally alone in the world—no home, no job, no relationship, and friends scattered across the land. I couldn't make a relationship work, it seemed, no matter what I did. I had failed in business. I couldn't see a reason to keep on living, and I no longer wanted to try. Tired of the struggle, I just wanted it all to go away and be over with.

But I'm luckier than that.

I've always been deeply spiritual, yet I'd lost my way and my faith along with it. It's not a coincidence that I found guidance in the middle of the bleak desert with not a soul around except me and God. It came as a mere whisper.

"You're not done here yet, Karen. You're going to be okay. Just keep going."

"I don't want to," I screamed back. "I'm so tired. I just can't do it anymore."

"Yes, you can," came the whisper. "You are not alone." In the sweet moment that followed, I knew in every fiber of my being that I wasn't and that I never had been alone. Guidance had been there all along.

I continued my journey toward Albuquerque—finally seeing the amazing red rocks of Sedona, through Oak Creek Canyon to Flagstaff, and on to the Grand Canyon. It's hard to lose sight of God in places like that.

Mary Alice opened up her heart and home to me when I arrived in Albuquerque in time to house-sit. After she returned from her trip, she offered to let me stay with her while I figured out if I wanted to live in Albuquerque or not. My bedroom overlooked the city and the amazing Sandia Mountains. I literally felt like I'd landed in paradise. I began to take day trips to Chaco Canyon, Bandelier, and Canyon de Chelly. When the spirits of the ancient ones at Chaco Canyon whispered to me, I knew that New Mexico was where I needed to be for the next stage of my growth.

One week led to the next. I found some freelance work, but no permanent job prospects. Four months later, I was down to my last $100 and was about to make plans to go to my parents' home in Florida with my tail between my legs to figure out what was next when I finally landed a job. I was able to get my own apartment, buy some furniture, and begin to make a life for myself in my new home state.

I began folk dancing, something I'd fallen in love with twenty-five years before and given up because my other partners didn't dance. One night, about a month later, a man walked into dance class. He was adorable—and a great dancer, too. His name was Gary. We were introduced and went out together later. At dinner that night, I decided that Gary was nice but he probably wasn't for me. He was so quiet that I did most of the talking, so I concluded that we didn't have much in common.

That's when I heard the whisper: "Karen, give this one a chance."

Two years later, Mary Alice was the matron of honor at our wedding.

Today I am blessed with a loving husband with whom I have many things in common, loving parents, loving friends, good health, a beautiful home that Gary and I built together, and most of all, happiness and peace of mind. I know now that even when we lose our way and our faith, we're not alone—we just think we are.

I suspect I was being spoken to all along, only I wasn't listening. Today I look forward to my alone time so that I may get quiet and wait—for the whispers that ensure me a more gentle path.

KAREN WALKER

QUE SERÁ SERÁ

Normally, *I would have called my mother after the* day I'd had at the office. I found myself on the other end of a project that had gone poorly, and by the end of the day I was battle weary and ready to move to a quiet little tree house in the country and open up a lemonade stand. I don't cry easily, but spent the evening fighting a large lump wedged in my throat like a thick stone. Thinking about Mom, her understanding and how she always knew the right thing to say, loosened the floodgates, and I cried like I hadn't since her death two years before.

I ended my evening curled up on the couch under a thick quilt in front of a John Wayne classic. What I really wanted was Doris Day, something sweet and happy to shake off this funk.

The next morning, I arrived at work early and chatted with Robin in the office next to me. Robin and I had worked together for two years, and she knew about my mom's death. She told me she'd been on a bike ride the previous night and was thinking about my mother and me.

"I don't know whether to tell you this, but . . ." Robin looked down at her desk and fidgeted with a paper clip. "Your mother gave me a message to pass on to you."

Robin had never known my mother, so I was a bit puzzled that Mom had used her to tell me something. On the other hand, Robin has similar spiritual beliefs.

"What did she say?" I asked, eager to know.

" 'Everything will work out. I love you.' "

My eyes brimmed with tears. I told Robin about the previous

evening, and we figured out that her conversation with Mom and my meltdown occurred at about the same time.

"I wanted proof that I was really talking to your mother," Robin explained, "so I asked her to tell me her maiden name, but I couldn't understand what she was saying. Then, just as abruptly as she started talking, she stopped."

I leaned against the door frame and thought about Robin pedaling along, Mom on her shoulder.

"The weird part is right after your mom stopped talking, this song popped into my head and kept playing over and over."

"What song?"

" 'Que Será, Será,' " Robin said.

A flood of vibrating warmth started in the soles of my feet and moved up my legs, stomach, chest, and into my face. I started crying.

" 'Que Será, Será' was one of Mom's favorite songs," I said. "She sang it to me all my life. She used that phrase like a mantra. Whatever will be, will be." I shook my head and smiled.

The look on my face was all the proof Robin needed to believe that she had truly participated in a divine encounter with my mother. She started crying, too, and stood to hug me. My burdens lifted in a cathartic flash. Suddenly, I could breathe easier. I felt light and airy and incredibly happy. I wanted to dance the hallways, renewed in my sense of peace and confidence. I always assumed Mom was up there watching over me, and now with her presence established through Robin, I feel as though she is truly here at my side.

Every once in a while when Robin and I are taking a break, or pass each other in the hall, I can't help but ask, "Have you heard from Mom lately?"

CAMMIE WALKER

LIFE'S LITTLE IRONIES

*That is the best—to laugh with someone because
you both think the same things are funny.*

GLORIA VANDERBILT

MATERNAL INSTINCTS GONE SOUTH

*S*arah came into our committee meeting carrying a small plastic pail lined with foam rubber and layered with facial tissue.

"I didn't have a babysitter," she announced. A gentle smile filled her face as she reached her small-boned hand into the pail and began stroking.

We looked more closely. A tiny peep rose from the Kleenex, identifying Sarah's "baby" as a fledgling bird. Her cat had brought the infant home after a nighttime trophy hunt.

Thinking the baby bird was dying, Sarah had put it in a little warm water to make its last moments more comfortable. Instead, the bird began to recover.

Sarah, a longtime public-health nurse whose compassion had not retired when she had, went into action. She offered blueberries and raspberries (a royal treat, in my opinion), which he rejected.

Next, using her computer, she made an Internet connection with Tri-State Bird Rescue and Research in Delaware. Here she learned what to feed Bird. The new diet consisted of three to four dropperfuls of applesauce and kitten food mixed with egg yolk every twenty-five to thirty minutes all day. At night the schedule eased slightly to every hour or so. Clearly, Sarah had taken the concept of demand feeding to new heights.

"I took him to church last Sunday," she said. "I had to. His next feeding was at eleven-fifteen A.M." She raised her doting eyes long enough to take in our surprise. "Oh, I was discreet about it. We sat in the back."

Bedtime was another challenge. I remember learning of a man who tied a string to his big toe and connected it to his infant daughter's cradle so he could rock her back to sleep at night if she woke. Sarah found a different solution. At night, the baby bird slept in a box with a screen over the top to keep the cat away. The box sat on the bed between Sarah and her husband.

Sarah was not the perfect mother. In the process of offering water, she almost drowned Bird. "I know now his windpipe is right below the tongue. The water got down in there. But I'm learning. Now I put the water in the applesauce."

Like any parent, Sarah was uncertain about her ability to cope with the challenges of the future. "The mother bird spends about two months teaching her babies how to find grubs on the ground. I don't know how I'm going to do that." She laughed.

At the next monthly committee meeting she reported with some confidence that Bird was growing nicely and now could be identified as a beautiful robin.

It was two months before I remembered to ask for an update. In the interim, Bird had been spending his weekdays at the family's store, where she could chalk up flight hours.

"At first he made little hops and low circles, but each time I let him loose, he flew a little higher. Then one day when I let him out, I forgot the fan was on. He flew right into it. I was devastated."

We all made sympathizing sounds—and exchanged guarded glances when Sarah responded, "Someone just brought me a baby kitten."

BETSY HUMPHREYS

Being popular is important.
Otherwise people might not like you.
MIMI POND

CHOCOLATE BLUES

It was the eve of St. Valentine's Day, and life was good. The book *Chocolate for a Lover's Heart* had hit the local bookstores and my doorstep, and there, on page 45, was my short story, a brilliant literary masterpiece for all lovers to share and weep over.

A small, elegant shop in the city where I live offered to host a book signing for me, and I was overjoyed at the prospect. Could a Pulitzer be far behind?

The shop was a magical place that sold images of angels of all types and styles, imported soaps, antique wall hangings, silk flowers, lace table runners, and a myriad of other wonders. It also smelled good.

Press releases were sent out, and my name and the name of the book were prominently displayed in the store's newspaper ads. I asked Julie, the gentle proprietor of the shop, about crowd control and extra security. She gave a wry laugh and assured me that she could easily handle the swarm of fans expected for the event. I was comforted by her show of confidence.

The day arrived, and I showed up for my date with destiny dressed in red, with a case of books and a heart-shaped box of chocolates. The signing table was set next to a window seat piled high with tapestry pillows, silk ribbons, sachets, and a sleeping gray cat. I artfully arranged a stack of books, uncapped my red signing pen, opened the box of chocolates, and waited for the hordes to rush in to meet me.

Twenty minutes into the signing, no one had entered the store. I strolled over to the complimentary refreshment table that had been set up in my honor and partook of a cup of hazelnut-flavored coffee and an oversized chocolate chip cookie. Browsing through the store, I saw a Native American angel doll, an angel lapel pin, and some angel greeting cards that I couldn't live without. I gave them to Julie to hold until after my signing.

Back at the table, I practiced signing my name with different inscriptions, wishing all the while that I'd sent out invitations. I was shaken out of my reverie by the sight of a customer entering the store.

The lone woman shopper slowly made her way to my area, stopping here and there, sniffing this and that. I smiled and tried to make eye contact. She looked over at the table and the stack of books and kept on walking.

I glared at her back, willing her to turn around. She continued to finger all the miniature silver frames on a shelf, ignoring my mental begging. My mind was a swirling pool of prayers: the Lord's Prayer, Feng Shui, Reiki, the secret Masonic creed, the Pledge of Allegiance. *Wait, she's turning around. She's heading my way. She's looking at the table. She's looking at the box of chocolates on the table. She's taking a chocolate from the box. She's walking away.*

I was thinking of throwing a half-nelson on her and retrieving my chocolate when another customer walked in. It was my friend Margaret. She stayed thirty minutes, talked and laughed with me, and pretended to be a crowd. At the end, she bought five books. I may leave her something in my will.

It was time for another cup of coffee and a cookie; signing five books can take a toll. Inspired, I took out my cell phone and called another friend.

My friend Melanie pulled up in her Jaguar a few minutes later. This would be the equivalent of a candy store for her. We chatted and made a lunch date, and then, true to form, she bought $136 worth of candlesticks and scented candles and forgot to buy a book.

Meanwhile, back at the table, there was some sudden activity. The cat had awoken, jumped on the table, and was enjoying a long stretch. A customer went over and started petting the cat and looking at one of the books. Why hadn't I thought of that before? Why didn't I just wake up the damn cat two hours before?

I scurried back to the table and took my seat. The person in front of me was petting the cat, reading the book, and eating a chocolate, all at the same time. I liked her immediately. She bought three books, and I signed them with a flourish. I was so delighted with her purchase that I invited her to lunch—my treat, of course.

The book signing was finally over, and it was time to do some serious business accounting. After payments to Julie for the merchandise I had set aside, and lunch for my customer, I had a net loss. *Now, let's see, all I have to do is save up, and I can afford another book signing.*

A few days later I saw Julie at a local café.

"We've sold out of your books," she said. "Can you bring in another order?" *Sold out?*

"Sure." I beamed, trying to hide my surprise. *It must have been the angels,* I thought, *or the cat.* Whatever it was, I realized that in spite of all my frantic efforts to merchandise the books, a lover's heart will always find its own way.

CLAUDIA McCORMICK

JUST KIDDING

Q: "What's the difference between a terrorist and
   a menopausal woman?"
A: "You can reason with the terrorist."

*I*t was my *time a few years ago. After going through a
dark year of the soul with hormones bouncing off the
ionosphere,* I had a hysterectomy. When I hit menopause,
everything went nuts—my weight, my endocrine system, and
my psyche. My waistline bloated, my brain became gray Jell-O. I
cried one minute and laughed the next.

I knew I was in full-blown menopause the night I turned up
the air-conditioning while my husband pulled a quilt over him.
"Don't even think about turning that down," I yelled. "I'm out of
estrogen, and I do have a gun."

I decided that either I could make myself (and everyone else)
miserable, or choose another path. The latter seemed healthier.
After all, I had survived hardships and mastered struggles far
tougher than menopause, right? Armed with only a positive attitude, estrogen patches, and a library of self-help books, I determined to discover the humor behind the mystique.

I was not surprised to learn that menopausal women commit
more violent crimes than any other group. Another source said
that women in menopause who drink more than five cups of coffee each day are less likely to commit suicide, but the article

didn't mention murder. For those of us in menopausal madness, I offer the following:

- Embrace menopause as the time during your life that you get to try new things—like sleeping nude. With hot flashes keeping you up all night changing nightgowns, why bother with one at all?
- Keep ice water next to your bed, either to drink or to douse yourself.
- If your usual, pleasant temperament momentarily disappears, warn your husband not to engage in serious discussions in a room with sharp objects—like the kitchen.
- Allow yourself some grace. You might need that crying jag to quiet your nerves.

I'm not sure why we have to have menopause. Menopause gets the blame even if it isn't the culprit. If I'm just in a bad mood, my husband increases my irritability when he asks "Did you take your estrogen?" or when he warns my daughters "Don't mess with your mama."

I do know that when I get to heaven I want to ask God, "What's the big idea of allowing midlife crisis, menopause, and the empty-nest syndrome to come at the same time?" He'll probably laugh and say, "What's wrong with you, Sheila, can't you take a joke?"

SHEILA S. HUDSON

CITY SLICKER

My husband, *Steve, grew up in an eighty-year-* old, one-bathroom house in Boston. He rarely left the city much as a child, and he thought everyone lived with concrete city blocks, crowded from stacked houses crammed close together.

When we married and moved to Seattle, he saw the mountains, the water, the luscious green trees and landscapes, and indeed believed the Northwest's adage—this is God's country.

Like any man obsessed with a goal, he's spent all sixteen years we've lived here dreaming about creating the perfect castle. Endless hours went into reading design books and touring open houses, when finally a new development came up that seemed perfect. It was in the woods, yet close to the city; we hiked the whole area and decided it seemed like the ideal spot to build a house. The roads were not in at first, so we had to walk up a long hill to view our favorite site. Usually, we walked up together—Steve and me with one of us carrying our eighteen-month-old son, Jack.

On this particular night, I wasn't thrilled to walk up the quarter mile of steep grade hauling our son, so I volunteered to go up and see if anything new had happened in the last few days if Steve would stay below to watch Jack. Steve insisted he'd go instead—being kind of macho that way. Dad took off—a man with a mission to create a kingdom for his family.

Jack and I waited at the bottom of the hill in the car. After a while, he got fussy, so I took him out of the car seat and walked toward the hillside. I pointed out to Jack that Daddy was coming. And boy was he coming! Steve was running down the hill, carrying a nine-foot-long log! What a sight. He was still in his dress clothes, tie flying, as he raced toward us. My husband was yelling, and at first I couldn't hear what he was saying. Then a strange thought popped into my head, and I yelled, "Did you see the bear?" I vaguely remembered some silly story about a real live black bear being seen a few miles away. He screamed back, adrenaline flowing, "Get in the car, now!" I hopped back in with Jack, and Steve ran up to us, ditched the log, and jumped into the driver's seat, breathless and shaking.

It seems that a 400-pound black bear likes our lot, too. According to my husband, the animal looked quite content sitting on the grass. They made initial eye contact when Steve turned the corner around a big dirt mound and spotted the bear only a few yards away.

Steve, being a smart city slicker from Boston, said, "I kept my cool, walked backwards slowly, and didn't run until I was out of the bear's sight. Then I ran like hell." Understandably, this was a shock for a man who'd never even seen a cow until he was twenty-two years old.

We've decided that if we do build a house in this development, we'll have to get a wooden bear for the backyard so that Jack will always know who was there first.

ROBIN RYAN

A REAL CORKER
OF A DAY

*M*y first assignment as a teacher of physical education and hygiene was in 1925. I didn't know what to expect at the Rutherford B. Hayes School on the corner of Central Avenue and East Fortieth, in the toughest district of Cleveland. It was an "overage" school. My students were all girls from eight to sixteen years of age. Some had never attended a school, or had so little education that they could not read or write. Yet, I got along well with the girls, and from time to time I'd find small gifts on my desk with no names attached—a candy bar, a pretty handkerchief, a fancy Valentine.

Rose was a sweet, unspoiled, fifteen-year-old Italian girl who begged me to go home with her and meet her parents and little brother.

In those days, gym teachers wore tennis shoes, midi-blouses, and bloomers as a work uniform. I used a small patent leather suitcase to carry my work clothes home in to be washed.

One Friday afternoon, Rose was so insistent about having me meet her parents that I decided to do as she wished. Her home was only a block away from the school. When we arrived, I noticed all the windows were barred. "To keep out bad men," Rose explained. The door was opened by a stout lady in a snow-white apron who bubbled over with excitement. We went into the kitchen, which was warmed by a wood-burning stove. Rose's father stood up from the table and enthusiastically shook my hand. I sat down and Papa shoved a full glass of wine in front of me. Mama and Papa conversed fast and furiously in Italian.

"Are they fighting?" I asked Rose.

"Oh no." Rose laughed. "They are very happy that you came. That's the way they always talk."

Pietro, who was about four years old, kept asking for "Vino—vino." His father poured a large glass half full of wine, which the youngster held in both hands and drank right down as if it were water.

Rose gave me a tour of the rest of the house. It was absolutely meticulous. The parents' bed was most interesting. It was piled high with feather quilts. I remarked to Rose that when they went to bed, their heads must hit the ceiling.

Rose chuckled. "When they get into bed, they sink way down to the height of a regular bed." There was a ladder leaning against the bedpost that revealed the way they got up there.

We went back to the table in the kitchen. Every time I took a sip of wine, Papa would fill my glass to the brim again.

Feeling the effects of the wine and the heat of the stove, I realized I must leave soon. Mama's and Papa's voices raised an octave. As I got up to leave, Papa insisted I take a bottle of wine home with me. Rose opened my suitcase and carefully wrapped my clothes around the bottle for protection. She walked to the streetcar with me, thrilled that I had at last met her family.

I slid into a seat along the side of the streetcar, homeward bound, putting my suitcase on the floor between my feet. As it was nearing the rush hour, the crowd rapidly increased and passengers began standing in the aisle, holding on to the straps that hung from the ceiling. A huge man planted himself directly in front of me. Fifteen minutes before I would reach my stop, a large woman pushed herself down the aisle, almost shoving the man into my lap. To keep his balance, the man accidentally kicked my suitcase. I heard a faint, muffled thud.

Oh, Lord, I thought, *I hope that wasn't the cork popping out of the bottle.*

In no time, my fears were substantiated. The unmistakable odor was definitely noticeable. I sat stony-faced, not moving a muscle. The crowded streetcar was very warm, and the obnoxious smell became stronger by the minute. I was still some distance away from my stop when the passengers next to me and in front of me began to turn their heads in my direction, sniffing the air with disgusted grimaces.

I didn't want to get off the car and have to walk six blocks to my home with the suitcase. I also didn't want people to think I was the cause of that dreadful odor. So . . . I screwed up my face with disgust, wrinkled my nose, sniffed loudly, and stared right back at the accusing eyes.

When my stop arrived, I got up, grabbed my case, pushed through the crowd, and hurried to the door. I never was so glad to get off a streetcar in my life.

I threw the little black suitcase and its contents into the trash. I never did tell Rose that her father's gift to me was the reason I carried a brand-new suitcase to school the following week.

GRACIE CAUBLE

You will do foolish things, but do them with enthusiasm.
COLLETTE

OPEN UP!

As a very young bride, I was terribly nervous about my first OB/GYN exam. My doctor, a soft-spoken, good-looking young man, was very thorough. In addition to the routine pelvic exam, he listened to my heart and lungs, took my blood pressure, and even checked my ears, nose, and throat. A year went by, and I made an appointment for my second annual visit. Though still quite nervous, I was sure that I had the routine down pat. I sat on the edge of the examining table, heart pounding, in a thin paper gown, the opening in front as instructed. Both trembling hands were tightly clutched under my chin in an attempt to hold the flimsy robe together. My baby-faced doctor strode through the door and after a few pleasantries said, "Open up." I did just that—whipped open the front of my robe. His face suddenly crimson, he looked from me . . . to the floor . . . to his shoes. . . . After what seemed like an eternity of stunned silence, my last shred of dignity instantly vanished as my eyes widened in shock when they fell on the tongue depressor in his hand!

MARGARET J. (MIMI) POPP

MORE CHOCOLATE STORIES?

Do you have a short story you want published that fits the spirit of *Chocolate for a Woman's Soul,* or *Chocolate for a Woman's Blessings?* I am planning future editions using a similar format that will feature love stories, divine moments, overcoming obstacles, following our intuition, and humorous events that teach us to laugh at ourselves. I am seeking heartwarming stories of one to four pages in length that feed and lift the spirit, and encourage us to go for our dreams.

I invite you to join me in these future projects by sending your special story for consideration. If your story is selected, you will be listed as a contributing author, receive a one-time honorarium fee, and have a biographical paragraph about you included. For more information, or to send a story, please contact:

Kay Allenbaugh
P.O. Box 2165
Lake Oswego, Oregon 97035

<kay@allenbaugh.com>

For more information, please visit my Web site!

http://www.chocolateforwomen.com

CONTRIBUTORS

BURKY ACHILLES is an Oregon-based writer, editor, and mother of two teenagers. She's the recipient of a Walden Fellowship and Soapstone Residency for Women Writers. She's currently earning her master's degree in writing at Portland State University, and working on her first novel about growing up in Hawaii.

JENNY KREFTMEYER ALTHEN is just beginning her writing career, this being her second short story to be published. She is currently employed in manufacturing. Her number one priority is her daughter, Amanda, and of course she loves chocolate! She enjoys spending time with her family and friends, arrowhead hunting, writing, and the outdoors. She resides in New Haven, Missouri. (573) 237-4810. <Jennyalthen@Hotmail.com>

MARY M. ALWARD lives in Ontario, Canada, and has a grown daughter and two grandsons who are the lights of her life. She's had two stories published in the anthology *Gifts of Our Fathers,* as well as articles published in *True Story, True Life.* She is also a writer for Noah Says, an on-line database, and has a column in *Storymania.* (519) 752-3819. <dalward@sprint.ca>

PATRICIA ANAND is happily retired with her husband in her dream home on the water in California.

MELANIE ANDERSON-CASTER is a freelance writer and communications professional. She enjoys writing stories about special people. She and her husband have raised two children in Lake of the Pines, California, and have two more to go. She credits her husband as the best writer and editor she knows. (530) 268-1467. <Writemel@jps.net>

BETTY AUCHARD is a semiretired public school art teacher who specializes in the art of printing and dyeing fabric. Her articles on how to print with leaves and flowers have appeared in *Sunset* and *Threads* magazines. Her fiber art has appeared in *Imagery on Fabric* and *Transforming Fabric*, along with articles for the International Nature Printing Society, whose members foster the ancient art of printing with fish, plants, and other materials found in nature. *Making Journals* will also feature her watercolor leaf prints in travel journal form. These works were printed during several years of touring the country with her husband in a motor home and are dedicated to his memory. <btauchard@aol.com>

TANNIS BENEDICT grew up traveling all over the world as the child of air force parents. She and her husband, Brian Frankish, have a film development and production company, Frankish-Benedict Entertainment, in which they dedicate themselves to "stories of the heart." Her writing debut was a two-character play, *Timing Is Everything*, a romantic comedy produced in Los Angeles, where she lives. She also writes screenplays, short stories, and poetry, and has been an actress for over twenty years. Having lost a son in 1996, her faith in God and the power of prayer have blossomed and illuminated her spiritual path. <tannisb@aol.com>

SANDE BORITZ BERGER began writing as a young teenager because her letters amused her parents and "they finally heard me." For several years she got sidetracked in the corporate world, writing and producing promotional video programs, until finally returning to her passion. A poet, essayist, and fiction writer, her work appears in *Every Woman Has a Story*, published by Warner Books.

She is presently writing a novel about boredom and its consequences in suburbia. She lives on Long Island and Manhattan with her "first reader" husband, Steven, and has two extremely independent and hardworking daughters. <MurphyFace@aol.com>

VALENTINA A. BLOOMFIELD is a receptionist and switchboard operator who truly enjoys her job. She is a member of the National Library of Poetry, and her poetry has been published. She is a member of M.A.D.D. (Mothers Against Drunk Driving) in memory of her friend Teresa Lynn Olson. She donates her free time to helping others, volunteering for the Make-A-Wish Foundation and for Love Letters, which provides emotional support to children dealing with long-term or catastrophic illness. She's happily married to her husband, Keith, and enjoys being a family with her very special twelve-year-old stepdaughter, Jennifer, and their two beautiful cats. (707) 451-2490.

JENNIFER BOYKIN shares her Virginia home with her husband and their two sons. The theme of her work as a writer, speaker, and personal coach is "The Triumph of the Human Spirit," a legacy to which she has been committed since the tragic death of her infant daughter, Grace. Toward that end, she shares with others the principles of "Legendary Living," helping clients develop an integrated strategic vision and legacy plan. She has been published in the *Washington Post* and is currently writing her first book. To receive her complimentary E-mail column, contact: <Jennifer @LegendaryLiving.com> or www.LegendaryLiving.com

DEBRA AYERS BROWN is "Meredith's Mom" and the marketing director of Savannah Tech. She has a B.A. from the University of Georgia, a Master's of Business Administration, and recently received her Nonprofit Manager Certification. Debra has stories in four of the *Chocolate* sequels and in *Guideposts*. Debra is on the board of directors of Southeastern Writers Association. She is looking forward to more free time now that her husband, Allen, the former mayor of Hinesville, is "retired" from politics. (912) 876-4617.

NANCY BUTLER retired a few years ago with her husband, and they moved from northern Illinois to Wild Dunes, on the Isle of Palms, South Carolina. She spends her time writing, painting, and playing golf. She loves to travel; her last trip (not including evacuating when Hurricane Floyd hit the South Carolina coast) was to Antarctica. Her favorite place to visit is South Africa, followed closely by the Amazon. (843) 886-3393. <NButler236@aol.com>

MICHELE WALLACE CAMPANELLI enjoys the part she's playing in creating a national best-selling *Chocolate* series. She lives on the space coast of Florida with her husband, Louis. She is a graduate of Writer's Digest School and Keiser College. Author of *Hero of Her Heart*, published by Blue Note Books, and *Margarita*, published by Hollis Books, she finds writing to be her outlet for artistic expression. Currently she is working on the sequel to *Margarita*, short stories, and a movie deal. <mcampanelli@juno.com> or www.michelecampanelli.com.

TALIA CARNER is a novelist with three yet-to-be-published novels. Her theme is motherhood threatened by big government. Before writing full-time, she founded Business Women Marketing Corporation, a consulting firm whose clients were Fortune 500 companies, and was the publisher of *Savvy Woman* magazine. Active in women's civic and professional organizations, she teaches entrepreneurial skills to women and participated in the NGO women's conference in Beijing in 1995. Israeli born, she served in the army during the 1967 Six-Day War. She and her husband and four children live on Long Island, New York. <TalYof@aol.com>

GRACIE CAUBLE is deceased, but her memory lives on in her humorous stories. Living into her nineties, she ultimately continued writing by using Braille. She is survived by her husband, Al, and her story was contributed by her best friend of fifty years, Alice Hardman.

DEBBIE CLEMENT is a freelance writer. Her inspirational stories are primarily about family and travels. Her work has been published in a professional magazine and the *Atlanta Journal-Constitution*. Debbie resides with her husband and son in the Metro Atlanta area. <DLClement@atl.mediaone.net>

BARBARA DALBEY has been a fitness professional for fourteen years. Her passion for teaching has expanded to include corporate employee programs for wellness and self-image. Her mission is to re-educate and explore the fallacy of the word *diet* as she focuses on mind, body, and spirit. She enjoys reaching out to people through her teaching, lectures, and articles. (503) 452-7576. <bdalbey@teleport.com>

BARBARA DAVEY is an executive director at Christ Hospital in Jersey City, New Jersey, where she is responsible for public relations and fund-raising. She holds bachelor's and master's degrees in English from Seton Hall University. A service near to her heart is the Look Good, Feel Better program, which supplies complimentary wigs and cosmetics to women undergoing treatment for cancer. Her attitude toward life is "Expect a miracle!" She and her husband, Reinhold Becker, live in Verona, New Jersey. <wisewords2@aol.com>

ALBERTA JAMES DAW is a writer and an artist who lives in Kansas City, Missouri, with her architect husband. She is the current art editor for *Potpourri*, a literary magazine. In the past, she has been a producer of educational film strips, spent a summer excavating a Woodlands Indian site with a University of Missouri archaeological crew, and has been a teacher. She and her husband have reared five children who now are rearing families of their own in various cities throughout the United States.

KAREN C. DRISCOLL lives in Maryland with her husband of ten years and their three preschool children. While pregnant with her twins, she completed a master's degree in elementary and special education, and is currently a full-time mom. In the past year she has taken up writing as a creative outlet while her children nap. Several of her essays and poems have recently been accepted for publication in books and magazines. <kmhbr­driscoll@hotmail.com>

LAURIE HOPKINS ETZEL is an author, poet, freelance writer, and teacher. She writes children's books and nonfiction. Her children's story "Magic Memaw" appeared in *Come to the Gathering*. She is particularly interested in researching mythology and wolves. As a teacher, she has piloted several programs in the Austin Independent School District, and has presented at the Texas Middle School Conference and at the National Middle School Conference. Currently she is collecting Native American wolf myths for an anthology. <msetzel@hotmail.com>

CANDIS FANCHER, M.S., C.C.C., is a speech and language pathologist in a hospital setting. She integrates humor and "pleasure pause" strategies to enhance patient care, communication, and healing. Faith, family, and friends are her personal highest priorities. She lives with her husband, Duane, a pharmacist, and her children, Chad and Jill, who describe her as being "spontaneously weird." Her Inner Sources seminars, "Staying Afloat in the Stresspools of Life," entertain, inform, and inspire participants to Stop, Notice, Act, and Create heart-to-heart connections—as does her seminar, "Life Is Like a Bowl of Chocolates." She is the creator of a "Chocolate Chips" newsletter. (612) 890-3897.

HOLLY FEDAK has changed positions, moved, and recently married. She is the director of women's and children's services at Exempla St. Joseph's Hospital in Denver, Colorado, and is enjoying her new husband and her family. (303) 759-5954.

LUCI N. FULLER is an essayist whose work has appeared in magazines and books around the country. She is also the author of the nonfiction book *Where the Universe Breathes: Lessons from a Sacred Journey,* which her agent is now circulating. She lives in the scenic Pacific Northwest and welcomes writing assignments and other correspondence. (503) 492-4317. <LuciFuller@aol.com>

NANCY B. GIBBS is a weekly religion columnist for the *Cordele Dispatch* and a freelance writer for Honor Books. She has been published in newspapers, books, and magazines. She's a pastor's wife, Sunday school teacher, and writer. She won approximately 300 on-line contests over an eighteen-month period, including first place in the Chicken Soup for the Pet Lover's Soul contest and second place in the Amazing Animal Actors contest. She resides in South Georgia with her husband, Roy. <DAISEY DOOD@aol.com>

AERIAL GILBERT is a graduate of Guide Dogs for the Blind, Inc., and is now its director of volunteers at the San Rafael, California, campus. She manages a vibrant volunteer staff of 450, comprising forty different positions. She is the vice president of the board of directors of the Earle Baum Center of the Blind in Santa Rosa, California. She is a registered nurse with a Bachelor of Science degree in biology. She and Deanne can be contacted at Guide Dogs for the Blind, Inc. (800) 295-4050, or <agilbert@guidedogs.com>.

BRENDA GRANT lives in Kansas City, Missouri, with her three children, Duggan James, Jordanna Marie, and Kiarra Delanie. She has worked in the "corporate jungle" in the health care computing solutions industry for twenty years. She also has a side interest as a massage therapist, with dreams of moving in a more holistic direction as part of her next life chapter. She is delighted to be published in *Chocolate,* knowing it will open up another new and exciting path. Amid the chaos of her normal life, she is passionate about seizing life's many moments and remembering to laugh often, love deeply, and live every day to the fullest. (816) 452-2984

DONNA HARTLEY is an international speaker, member of the National Speakers Association, change specialist, and survivor of a DC-10 plane crash. Owner and founder of Hartley International, she has been featured on NBC, ABC, PBS, the Learning Channel, and in the *New York Times.* Her popular book, video, and audio training series is called "Get What You Want." She is the author of *Fire Up Your Life—With a Wise Man, a Mentor and an Angel.* (800) 438-9428

EMILY SUE HARVEY, author and speaker, planned to be an English teacher, but the tragic death of her eleven-year-old daughter, Angie, changed all that. Writing, begun as therapy, soon became a passion. Years of pouring mind and soul onto paper focused her on what life is and is not about—and that relationships are the greatest thing going. She's convinced that, along with love, compassion makes the world go around. Her insights have converged into fiction and nonfiction upbeat stories and novels whose themes ring of triumph in the face of adversity. She is working on *God Only Knows,* a fictional mainstream novel about the struggles of a clergyman and his wife, and a book featuring warm family anecdotes titled *Flavors.* <EmilySue1@aol.com>

SHEILA S. HUDSON, founder of Bright Ideas, is a freelance writer and speaker living in Athens, Georgia. An award-winning writer, she enjoys credits in *Christian Standard, Lookout, Reminisce, Athens Magazine, Teddy Bear Magazine, Just Between Us,* and *The Pastor's Family.* She and Tim have been married over thirty years, and they have two daughters and three grandchildren. She and Tim have been at the Christian Campus Fellowship at the University of Georgia since 1982. (706) 546-5085. <sheila@naccm.org>

BETSY HUMPHREYS is a writer and community volunteer. She and her husband live in the Blue Ridge foothills of North Carolina, where she scribbles creative nonfiction and poetry to her heart's content. Her work has appeared in the *Charlotte Observer, North Carolina Literary Review, Muse and Spirit,* and other publications.

ANTIONETTE VIGLIATURO ISHMAEL is the sixth-grade teacher at Visitation Catholic School in Kansas City, Missouri. She was a 1997 recipient of the Excellence in Teaching Award in Missouri. She is also a writer, coach, the wife of Phil, and most of all . . . the proud mother of Patrick, Anthony, and Dominic.

NIKKI JENKINS's story was written for her by her friend Michele Wallace Campanelli.

JUDITH BADER JONES was born in upstate New York and reared in Missouri. She is a former psychiatric nurse, an avid organic gardener, a cook, and a mother. Her poetry, Flower Girl photos, and short stories have been published in both commercial and literary publications. (913) 831-2074. <fowler314@msn.com>

LINDA L. S. KNOUSE is a freelance writer. Her feature articles have appeared in all sixteen publications printed by Montgomery Newspapers in the greater Philadelphia area, as well as in its *Lifestyles* magazine. Although her writing focus is primarily about life in the 1950s, she has also written animal rescue stories and written and edited for various dog interest groups. <col lies@email.msn.com>

DAWN KREISELMAN is a poet and short story writer. She lives in Florida with her husband, Ben, and her children, Eve and Teelah. Her hobbies include playing guitar, working out, and just having fun with her kids.

CHRISTI KROMMINGA is a freelance writer residing in Monticello, Iowa, where she is an avid journalist for her family of five, including three children. She especially enjoys recounting the emotions and blessings in the day-to-day celebration of Motherhood! (319) 465-5347

PENNE J. LAUBENTHAL, Ph.D., is coordinator of the Humanities Unit at Athens State University (Alabama), where she teaches courses such as Literature: The Healing Art, and Myth: Ritual and Culture. She is a former executive board member of the National Association of Poetry Therapy, and she serves on the advisory board of *Mythosphere*. She is certified in Reiki and in Integrative Yoga Therapy. Her article "A Humanist Looks at the Mind-Body Connection" appeared in the *Journal of the Medical Association of Georgia*. She offers workshops and seminars in bibliotherapy and mind-body healing. (256) 729-6500. <penneelk@aol.com>

KATHRYN LAY is a freelance writer and author living in Texas with her husband and daughter, two dogs, and a turtle. She has had over 300 articles, essays, and fiction pieces published for children and adults in magazines and anthologies, including *Chicken Soup for the Mother's Soul, Stories for the Family's Heart, Boys' Life Magazine, Woman's World, Guideposts,* and the children's anthology *A Glory of Unicorns*. She speaks on writing to children in schools and to writers at conferences. She can be reached at (817) 795-9413. <rlay15@aol.com>

CLAUDIA MCCORMICK, a weekly columnist for a metropolitan newspaper for the past ten years, is a former legislative aide to the president of the California State Senate and is presently running for public office. She is a world traveler and freelance writer, and is currently writing a mystery romance novel. She and her husband, Tom, live in Dublin, California, and share a combined family of seven children, eight grandchildren, and four stray cats. <Chindidub@aol.com>

ELIZABETH MCGINLEY is a homemaker and freelance writer/editor specializing in family and medical issues. Her favorite topic is life with her husband and her two daughters in a big old house in Philadelphia.

JANELL DAVIS MATHEWS is a writer, an editor, and a newspaper opinion columnist. She holds a B.A. in English from Utah State University. She feels truly blessed to be Connor's mom, Trent's wife, and is grateful to live in a place where she is surrounded by her extended family as well. <tmathews@favorites.com>

DEBORAH MILLS-ELDER is a freelance photographer in her spare time, a catcher for the "All-Ontario" provincial softball team, and works full-time at Queen's University in Battersea, Ontario, Canada, as a compensation administrator. She sees rearing her children as her biggest accomplishment in life, and her grandparents were the most influential people in her childhood. <millsd@post.queensu.ca>

AMY MUNNELL has been a freelance writer/editor since 1987. She is on the Southeastern Writers Association board of directors and edits its newsletter, "Purple Pros." She and Kia have been partners since 1997. She lives in Athens, Georgia. (706) 354-0361. <72172.3417@compuserve.com>

KATE MURPHY lives on Skaneateles Lake in upstate New York. Writing is a second career for her after many years working with women and their children. Much of her work focuses on living with illness and disability, and as a former Judson Jerome Scholarship winner, she has published poetry and personal essays exploring these themes. She is a survivor of breast, ovarian, and colon cancers, and is currently working on a book about emotional support and cancer recovery. <katemm@mind spring.com>

CAROL NEWMAN grew up in southwest Oklahoma among spirited, and spiritual, women. It is of these women, and for these women, she writes. A frequent contributor to *Guideposts* and *Angels on Earth* magazines, she now resides in Leawood, Kansas, with her husband, Tom.

JANICE NORMAN lives in the Smoky Mountains of North Carolina, teaches writing classes, and loves life. She's written *A Woman's Journal,* a workbook for women in recovery, as well as many feature stories and humorous essays. She lives with her husband of thirty-eight years, one dog, and two cats. <norbob jan@aol.com>

CLARA OLSON is a pastor with a degree in Christian education. Her work of ministry to children and families is a model and inspiration internationally. For church leaders, she has written a book, *How Do Children Fit into the Meta-Church Model,* and many articles and teacher lessons for volunteers in children's ministries. She is a popular speaker at church growth conferences, women's retreats, and parent training seminars. She is a Certified Parent Effectiveness Training (P.E.T.) instructor. Clara is wife to Rod (for thirty-three years) and mom to Cindy and Erik. She is grandmother to Danielle, Brandyn, Tera, Kaleb, and Kaden. (541) 593-6002. <Rod-Olson@MSN.COM>

TARA GLENNON OTT is a human resources coordinator for a national retail organization, but her dream is to make writing her career. A native of Shamokin, Pennsylvania, she now resides in Massachusetts with her husband and is currently working on a book that she hopes to publish. <taradon@att.net>

DEBBIE PETRICEK, M.S., M.N.L.P., is founder of In Potentia: Center for Creativity and Development, in Portland, Oregon. With passions for psychology, art, and communication, she promotes the importance of creativity in everyday life and imagery in health and wellness. In a playful and productive forum she encourages creative expression, learning, and development in order to support desired changes in success, health, and creativity. Privately or in small groups, participants develop invaluable insights, skills, and behaviors for a lifetime of growth and change. (503) 226-9161. <dpetricek@earthlink.net> or <//home.earth link.net/~dpetricek/>

MARGARET J. (MIMI) POPP operates a day-care center. She lives in Bel Air, Maryland, with her husband of thirty years; two children, Jaime and Joe; their dog; and three cats. She writes personal essays, short stories, and travel articles, and hopes to one day find the time to write a novel. She enjoys traveling, reading, wine tastings, and gourmet meals prepared by her husband. She cherishes those rare evenings when everyone is seated at the dinner table. <MMIMPOP@CS.COM>

LINDA RESH recently retired from Sarasota's public schools and remains on staff at the Child Protection Center, where she serves as a group facilitator treating families of sexually abused children. Her creative writing is lifted from the pages of her personal journals. Here she records everything from her life experiences—special moments, hurts, and a search for meaning that brings clarity to her spiritual journey. Her greatest joy and teacher is her daughter, Paige, who recently presented her with her first grandchild, Nathan Thomas. He's her latest passion and inspiration as they together capture the wonders of life with new eyes. <Regal2fish@aol.com>

RUTH ROCKER is a part-time personnel manager and former director of the YMCA Adult Literacy Program in New Orleans. She and her husband, Henry, have seven children, one special angel, and seventeen grandchildren. Christianity is an integral part of her life, and she currently fills the role of "Granny" for Granny's Angels, a group of youth dedicated to performing Christian service in the community. She recently moved from a large metropolitan area to a small rural community outside the city, where her dream is to pursue her inspirational writings. <rrocker@1-55.com>

CAROLE R. ROTSTEIN was born in Sydney, Australia. She is an aspiring writer and experienced speaker, now dreaming of "proofreading the world" with her passion for correct spelling and grammar. She is learning to live a different life, consciously creating daily joy, and looking for opportunities to reach out to others in grief. Her story is dedicated to Rachel and Joshua, and to Linda Moore Browning, Beverly Lauck, Marcia Liberson, and Evelyn C. Nast, four steadfast women who guide her on her healing path. (503) 245-5680

ROBIN RYAN is one of the nation's foremost career authorities and is the best-selling author of five books: *24 Hours to Your Next Job,*

Raise or Promotion: *Winning Resumes*; *Winning Cover Letters*; *60 Seconds & You're Hired!*, and *Job Search Organizer*. She has appeared on over 400 TV and radio programs, including *NBC Nightly News with Tom Brokaw* and *Oprah*. She has been featured in *Money, Newsweek, Glamour, Fortune, Woman's Day, Cosmopolitan, McCall's*, the *Wall Street Journal*, and *USA TODAY* in addition to writing a career column for the *Seattle Times*. A popular national speaker, she also has a private career counseling practice in Seattle. (425) 226-0414

SUZY RYAN lives in Southern California with her husband and three small children. Her articles have appeared in *Woman's World, Today's Christian Woman, The American Enterprise, Focus on the Family, USA Today,* and various newspapers. <KenSuzyR@aol.com>

JUDI SADOWSKY is a writer who has done television and magazine work. She has been married for thirty-four years to the love of her life and has two fabulous children and one amazing daughter-in-law. She is currently working on a book of essays and patiently waiting for her first grandchild to be conceived. <jsadowsky@earthlink.net>

JEAN SCHNEIDER is retired and lives in York, Nebraska. She writes primarily to record a family history for her four grandsons. (402) 362-4778

ROBIN MICHELLE SILK, M.S., C.C.C., is a speech and language pathologist in the public schools. She specializes in working with the preschool and elementary population. She has had her poetry appear in *Womankind, In Friendship's Garden,* and *This Is My Beloved*. She lives with her best friend and husband, Alfredo; two wonderful children, Christian and Brandon; and loyal cat, Rio, in San Carlos, California. She feels so blessed to have the love and support of her families and friends. <mllelapin@aol.com>

ALAINA SMITH is a writer. Although her jobs have included newspaper editor, training coordinator, and office manager, writing will always be her primary passion. Hoping to make the transition from writer to author, she is currently working on her first novel. Her priorities are friendship, family, laughter, and living up to her personal goals. She is a displaced Oregonian, and currently lives in Seattle, Washington, with her loving and supportive husband, Frank. (206) 368-9920

DEBRA SMITH is a mail carrier who moved to Colorado after graduating from Michigan State University. She lives on five acres outside of Parker, Colorado, with five cats in the house, a feral cat in the barn, four dogs, three chickens, two ducks, two horses, and an occasional family of skunks. In her spare time, she volunteers at the Maxfund Animal Shelter. Recently she rode in the Multiple Sclerosis 150-Mile, Two-Day Bike Ride fund-raiser.

SHEILA STEPHENS is an international award-winning poet, writing teacher, columnist, and speaker who enjoys helping people build their lives "from the inside out." To her, self-esteem is a spiritual journey of accepting the seed of love that divine spirit places in each heart. She's just completed *Light Up Your Dreams with Love* and *Walking with the Flowers: Insights and Inspiration from a Softer Place,* which honor this intent. <joywriters@uswest.net>

FRANCINE M. STOREY is a poet and playwright, and her writing has recently been seen Off-Off Broadway in American Voices, Actors' & Writers' Workshop, Classical Forms, and Modern Voices. A book of poems, *Dead in the Snows of Love,* has been filmed by Vox Theatre Company. Her other work has been produced by the Abingdon, the Pulse, and the Impact Theatre Companies. Publications include *The Journal of Irish Literature, The Art and Craft of Poetry,* and *By Actors, for Actors, Volumes I, II, and III.*

Judy Torres is a professional recording artist of fourteen years. She is best known for her hits "No Reason to Cry" and "Come into My Arms," which received national radio airplay and charted on Billboard's dance charts. Her albums, "Love Story" and "My Soul," debuted her video, "I Love You for All Seasons." She performs in nightclubs nationwide. When in New York's tri-state area, she's a radio personality on the KTU 103.5 FM morning show, Monday through Friday, six to ten A.M. and Sunday nights from nine to midnight. She models plus-size fashions for Ashley Stewart and Hanes, for which she appeared on *Good Day NY.* She resides in New Jersey. (212) 647-1575 or (201) 222-1353

Paula J. Toynbee is proud to have obtained her goal of becoming a correctional officer in 1991. She enjoys the many challenges that it brings her. She is happily married to James (her "guardian angel"). They live in rural Vacaville, California, on three acres with their four children. Her newest challenge is to pursue her passion of writing, and she hopes someday to write of the joys of her "blended" family. Fax: (707) 448-6900

Mari Pat Varga is a speaker, educator, and coach. She travels internationally, presenting workshops and seminars on how to be an excellent communicator. She is the author of *Great Openings and Closings* and *The Presenter's Journal: A Tool for Making Presentations Memorable.* She has inspired, entertained, and challenged business audiences since 1985. (773) 989-7348. <mari pat@vargacom.com> or Web site www.vargacom.com

Kim Dixon Waldman is a former Texas bank executive. She currently resides in Scottsdale, Arizona, with her husband, Neal; son, Zachary; and daughter, Kelsey. This is her first publication, and she hopes to write many more. <nkwaldman@cs.com>

CAMMIE WALKER lives with her eight-year-old daughter, McKenna; life partner, Jim; and their dog, Susitna, in Anchorage and Kashwitna Lake, Alaska, where she works as a cost accountant (to fill the cupboards) and a writer (to fuel the soul). She is currently collaborating on a children's novel with McKenna. <cammieak@yahoo.com>

KAREN WALKER has twenty years of experience as a public relations professional writing marketing plans, brochures, newsletters, feature stories, annual reports, and press releases for a variety of clients. She began personal journal writing in 1978 as part of her spiritual quest for healing. She has been working on improving her self-esteem most of her adult life, and is currently working on her first nonfiction book, *I'm Nobody, Will You Listen Anyway? . . . How I Learned to Love Myself.* She resides in Albuquerque, New Mexico, with her husband, Gary, and their dog, Wolf. (505) 344-1387. <kgwalker@flash.net>

ANNIE WILSON is a wife, mother, and stepmother who lives in Phoenix, Arizona. She enjoys reading, scrapbooking, playing the piano, and writing for self-expression. She retired as a school secretary in Idaho to move to Arizona and marry Bud, her teenage sweetheart. With her belief that family history should be passed on, she recently finished a family history book, complete with text and pictures, beginning with her great-great-grandparents up through each of her children's lives. (602) 788-9597. <anniew@mciworld.com>

MYRA WINNER was born and bred in Georgia and has recently returned to the Deep South after a decade up north, along the Delaware River. She currently lives on Amelia Island, a barrier island off the Georgia/Florida coast. Her belief in the power of story led her to create *Tale Tellers,* a spiral-bound, brightly colored, twelve-page book/kit that enables you to write your own story using photographs. She has recorded eleven of her stories on a cassette called *Caviar and Moonshine*. She is also writing her first novel—the working title is *Good Morning Glory*. Both *Tale Tellers* and *Caviar and Moonshine* are available by calling (904) 491-3300, or through <winsedge@aol.com>.

LEE ANN WOODS is a feature commentator for the award-winning National Public Radio affiliate, WNCW, in Spindale, North Carolina, and a children's librarian. Her stories and articles have appeared in various periodicals, and her first children's picture book, *Grandpa Whitt's Grocery*, published by Chapter & Verse Publishing for Children, is scheduled for release in 2000. She grew up hearing many stories in her Tennessee mountain home, which became a focus in her writing. Bright Mountain Books will be publishing her stories and thoughts on life from the southern Appalachians. She now lives in the mountains of Asheville, North Carolina, with her husband and their two sons, Gabriel and Blaise. <Leeawoods@aol.com>

ACKNOWLEDGMENTS

I gratefully acknowledge the "Chocolate Sisters" for sharing their powerful, poignant, and heartwarming stories of love, motherhood, divine moments, compassion, healing journeys, and humor. Their true tales are, indeed, blessing the world.

My untold thanks for all the devotion given to the *Chocolate* series from Caroline Sutton, senior editor; and her assistant, Nicole Diamond, at Fireside/Simon & Schuster; and to the powers that be: Mark Gompertz, Trish Todd, Christine Lloreda, Sue Fleming Holland, Lisa Sciambra, Megan Curren, and Cynthia Kirk; and to all those other Simon & Schuster chocolate lovers who are working behind the scenes. I am truly grateful to have so much talent focused on the *Chocolate* series.

Kudos to my agent, Peter Miller of PMA Literary and Film Management, Inc., and his chocolate-loving staff, Delin, Elaine, and Kate. Thanks to Peter, the *Chocolate* series is inspiring women around the world.

Closer to home, my deepest appreciation and respect to Burky Achilles for her editing expertise, friendship, and nudges that keep me going to yoga classes.

As always, I offer my undying affection to my one-in-a-million husband, Eric; our delightful grown sons and their wives; and our true-blue friends. Just as the stories in *Chocolate for a Woman's Blessings* convey, there is no higher blessing than to love and be loved.

ABOUT THE AUTHOR

Kay Allenbaugh is the author of *Chocolate for a Woman's Soul; Chocolate for a Woman's Heart; Chocolate for a Woman's Heart and Soul; Chocolate for a Lover's Heart; Chocolate for a Mother's Heart; Chocolate for a Woman's Spirit;* and *Chocolate for a Teen's Soul.* She resides in Lake Oswego, Oregon, with her husband, Eric Allenbaugh, author of *Wake-Up Calls: You Don't Have to Sleepwalk Through Your Life, Love or Career!*

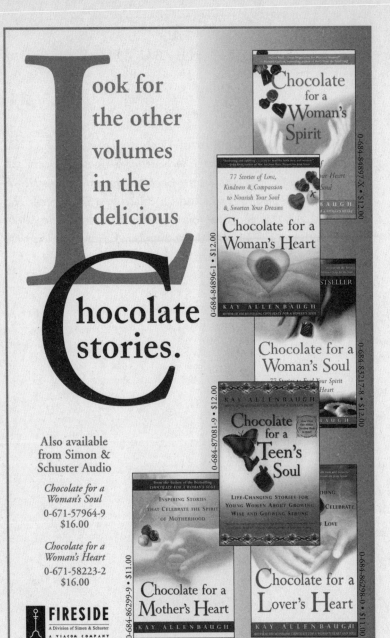